MASTERING THE PhD PROCESS
Like A
NINJA

A Holistic Approach To Organizational Techniques Essential Time Management Skills, And More: The TLC WAY

BY
Tanya Lovejoy-Capers, PhD

Library of Congress Control Number: 2020915225

Paperback ISBN: 978-1-7355-3860-0
eBook ISBN: 978-1-7355-3861-7

The purpose of this book is to inspire and provide guidance for individuals to be successful in the PhD process.

The TLC Touch Publishing, LLC
400 Gilead Road #2052
Huntersville, NC 28078

"

Education is the key that unlocks knowledge and provides power...it is the biggest investment that you will make toward your future—one that my book will help you maximize!

TANYA LOVEJOY-CAPERS, PHD

Dedication

This handbook is dedicated to my brother Dr. Lovejoy, II. Dear Brother, you were the sensei and I was the grasshopper who learned that patience and persistence was key during my doctoral journey. It was because of you that I aspired to be the best learner that I could be. Your intelligence and knowledge allowed me to see a bigger part of the world through your eyes. I appreciated all the guidance and direction that you provided me so that I could succeed in meeting my goal of acquiring my PhD. I appreciate your telling me how proud of me you were. Words cannot express just how grateful I am to you. I will always cherish all the great memories that we shared. This grasshopper will carry the legacy now in your honor.

Love always, your Sis

Acknowledgement

Thank you to every person that has inspired, encouraged, supported, and empowered me throughout my journey. It is through your love, grace, and knowledge, that I am able to preserver through adversity.

I would like to acknowledge and express my deepest gratitude to the following people for their support and contribution in the creation of this book.

Thank you to the love of my life, my husband David who had the patience of Job while engaging me in the revision process. The wonderful family, friends, and colleagues: Latanya Gregory, Tamiko Lovejoy, Silean Eaaves, Dr. Yvette Clifton, Latonya Hicks, Dr. Linda Barbee, Rodrick Hollis, Greg Zar for their feedback. Ronda Harris for her editing and contribution to Steps fourteen and fifteen.

And finally, to my children, Day'ton, Jordan, and Andraea. To Day'ton who was patient each time I knocked on his door for advice, and to Jordan, who entertained my long conversations about the visions I had for my book, and my daughter Andraea for always pushing me to dig deeper into my soul to bring out my creativity.

Table of Contents

PREFACE

───────── ༺༚༻ ─────────

Over the last six years, I have come to realize that many online learners have been very confused when deciding how to manage their work based on their inability to use effective time management techniques. Individuals who use time management techniques from time to time can enhance those skills as workloads become more complex.

Although online learning allows adult non-traditional students to focus on their careers and families without sacrificing their education, institutions have forgotten these learners as younger students have infiltrated the market by foregoing brick and mortar options while attending college. Because of this shift in the original model, it has become overwhelming for adult non-traditional learners to maintain a healthy balance between family, work, and academic studies.

Universities and colleges are discovering that students are failing courses based on their inability to use effective time management skills. Usually, their failure is consistent with not completing the weekly responses to their peers. Consequently, this handbook has been developed to provide time-proven skills to assist with overcoming the challenges that online learners must conquer.

The handbook is broken down into an initial step, proceeded by fifteen steps that break down the process leading up to the dissertation procedures. Step one focuses on the plan of attacking the course material, step two concentrates on setting up and organizing your course room folders, and step three targets the tools necessary to create an organizational system to maintain the course materials. Step four explains the importance of having a strong support group, step five assists with the selection of the research topic, and step six reviews the Dissertation Research Plan (DRP). Step seven prepares you to take your comprehensive exam, and step eight establishes the ground rules for receiving IRB approval. Step nine gets you ready to participate in the dissertation course rooms, and step ten suggests ways to set up folders to keep you organized during this reiterative process. Step eleven prepares you for the interview phase of your data collection process, and step twelve illustrates the process of presenting your dissertation. Step thirteen offers you a quick reference guide to formatting proper in-text citations, along with the correct manner to cite your university sources. Step fourteen offers many handy computer tips and tricks to make your job easier, and step fifteen includes advice from graduate students who discovered there were better ways to approach their challenges, but no one had shared these little secrets before.

There is also a sample directory for keeping each folder's work at your fingertips and a tools section that describes useful aides to help develop your dissertation. In addition, there is a section of encouragement just in case you forgot your reason(s) for participating in a doctoral program. This handbook was created because I want you to be the best you that you can be by succeeding and hearing those all-important words,

"CONGRATULATIONS, Dr."

THE INITIAL STEP

Your Decision to Enroll in a PhD Program

———— ᕲ 6 ᕲ 6 ————

The initial step to conquering a PHD program is simply to think about yourself and to determine what goals you are trying to accomplish. Are you enrolling in a PHD program as a personal accolade, or are you using this milestone to enhance your professional career? The other important question that you will have to ask yourself is, "Do I have the time it takes to be successful with completing the program?" Advanced degrees are time consuming, especially if you must juggle a full-time job and other responsibilities.

You will become aware that attending any university is quite expensive. It can become a financial burden and may possibly be one that your family cannot afford to risk should you decide to withdraw from a program mid-stream. Once you can answer this question with certainty, the next step is to review all programs at universities that will assist with meeting your defined goals.

Do not just take the course description at face value. It is recommended that you speak with an experienced counselor at the selected university to discuss your reasons for choosing their program and to share your goals for attending their institution. This process can help determine if you have chosen the correct program that aligns with your projected goals. Consider whether the advisor you speak with is knowledgeable about the program you want to pursue. Ask yourself if this person is there to guide you toward a successful PhD or is that person a salesperson who is being paid to sell you useless coursework that only benefits the university's bottom line?

Don't be afraid to ask right upfront if the institution withholds coursework to arbitrarily set the student's pace. Some universities set limits on when each step in the course can be completed. This means you cannot work ahead, but must, for example, work on week 8 assignments only during week 8. Consider looking into programs that will honor their word to allow you to work at your own pace, according to your responsibilities and schedule. If you were attending a brick and mortar institution you have free access to complete all assignments at your pace and nothing would be withheld; your syllabus would show you what would be required reading for each week and the written assignments due. Nothing would keep you from reading or writing ahead, so this information should not be withheld from online coursework either.

If you are getting a PhD in order to enhance your chances of job advancement, for example, does your employer consider your university to be an accredited institution? Otherwise, your hard work will not be recognized.

In some fields of study, there are very specific requirements for a university program to be accredited. For instance, should you decide to pursue a degree in psychology, you should know if you are required to enroll in a program that supports hands-on clinical training, if your goal is to become a clinical psychologist and obtain your license. For your own professional and financial safety, you should know if your state's requirements for licensure align with the university's perspective program. Each state has different structured guidelines that you must adhere to in order to become licensed, and the state may not consider that the university you have chosen has an accredited program. When you have performed your due diligence and have had all your questions answered, now is the time to decide if the program is a good fit for you. If the answer is YES!, you are on your way to a very rewarding journey.

Now that you have decided to embark on this wonderful journey in your life, remember that there are financial assistance programs to help with your advanced education. If you are a military veteran, take advantage of your education benefits. Many institutions offer monetary aid in the form of scholarships, flexible programs with fixed tuition fees, government assistance, and, of course, the last resort are the various loan programs.

Ready, Set, go...Organization is the Key to Success

Your PhD program, as you know, does not begin with your dissertation. Therefore, before you even attempt to venture into this part of the curriculum, you will have a mountain of upfront preparation that you must do. The hardest part of starting a PhD program most students grapple with is the dreaded question of where do I begin? How do I stay on track? What is the best way to achieve time management? And how do I stay organized? Well, you are in luck, because I can answer these questions. I had to answer them for myself, and I want to share those answers with you. As an online learner, I successfully completed a Master's in Counseling with a 4.0 GPA and a PhD in Psychology with a 3.867 GPA.

The mention of my GPA is not to make anyone feel defeated. On the contrary, as a mature adult who decided to explore advancing my education later in my life, it is to encourage you, because if I can do it, I know and have faith that you can do it, too. I know this for sure because before I decided to take the plunge, I talked myself out of it on so many occasions because of the fear that I would fail. Normally, I am usually up for any challenge, and I usually face those challenges head on.

However, we are all very familiar with how other people's insecurities can become yours, based on how they are projected onto you. Luckily, I was at a place in my life when I had a come to Jesus moment with myself and told myself that I can face all fears, no matter how small or big they maybe. I felt that this was the only true way I could receive and appreciate the gifts that I had been fortunate to be blessed with by God. I developed an understanding that we are all vessels that have been given a huge role in life. We should determine what that role is and take up that challenge while we are here on earth. I decided mine was to enhance my abilities and gifts of counseling others.

One day as I was watching television, a commercial came on—one that I had seen many times before. The spokesperson said with authority, "What are you waiting for?" Right then, I asked myself out loud, "Yeah, what are you waiting for?" I immediately grabbed my laptop and began investigating online programs that would meet my goal to earn my PhD in psychology. I never looked back, and I ran full steam ahead, right into my academic advancement, that began with receiving a Master's Degree in Counseling.

I took one class at a time because I was working full-time. But I tell you this, the day of my graduation was one of the best days of my life. I mean, I walked across that stage with more than a sense of pride. I was vindicated! The smile that I had on my face, you could see around the world, that is how proud of myself, I was. I was so elated that my son said he was calling my name while he was standing in front of me as I exited the stage, and I heard nothing! I was in a state of euphoria. I could not believe that I had achieved something that many educators, years earlier, had discouraged me from pursuing. I tell you—I was not just scared to advance my education, I was frightened.

But on June 30, 2013, I proved everyone wrong. Not only did I complete my master's program, I finished with distinction, an honor that had been the furthest thing in my mind. This enlightened me; I realized that I had it in me to be a successful student. It motivated me to continue pursing my quest to achieve my PhD in psychology. Funny, but true, I was supposed to wait one year before attempting any more course work, but I was so determined and had a new sense of *self,* that I re-enrolled within less than three months in a PhD program.

So, I say to you—as a wife and mother of three children—if I can do it, so can you. Taking the first steps to enroll in a program is the major hurdle that you must conquer. The key to being successful in the program is organization. Luckily, I have you covered. Whether you are not the greatest with time management or feel that you do have some degree of skill at it, I can help you develop great tools to decrease or alleviate some of your stressors as you progress through your PhD program.

Notes

STEP ONE

Plan of Attack

Most online courses open three days prior to the official start of the semester. These three days are critical to get a jump on staying on track. I call this three-day period your *plan of attack* time. This is considered the plan of attack phase because this is when you strategically lay out your course work for the entire semester. The first step is to log onto your student account and open your curriculum. Study your university's calendar. Often this three-day period begins the Friday prior to the official start of class. During this plan of attack time, do the following:

1. Review your professor's expectations.

a) Here you will find all the requirements to complete your coursework.

b) The day/time that your work is due.

   1. Your weekly coursework will have an individual deadline during the week.

2. Your assignment/projects are typically due by Sunday, 11:59 pm.

c) Ask yourself what will happen if you have an emergency? Determine how to best handle family or work-related emergencies and still get your weekly coursework completed.

d) How do you contact your professor?

e) After reading the professor's list of expectations you will respond that you understand and agree with the terms.

f) This is also a good time to ask any questions or express any concerns. Be honest with yourself and your professor. Believe me—your professor will have already heard many worries that students express and will be aware of how to best meet your needs as a learner who is balancing work, family, and education. True educators want you to be successful.

2. Read your syllabus.

a) Here you will find all the required/optional course materials.

b) If you have not already done so, this is a great time to purchase these items.

c) Many universities ask students to write an introduction about themselves and what you hope to achieve by taking this course, according to the subject matter.

d) This is a great time to tackle this request and submit it to the course-room.

Helpful Hints:

1. Read ahead. It is always a good idea to purchase your course materials before school officially opens, even a couple of weeks before. This way, you can get a head start on the course readings.

Reading ahead allowed me to complete multiple assignments during the weekend before the course room officially opened. I would also use the first week of school to complete any additional work that my schedule allowed. I could prepare up to two weeks of work at a time by using that method. This is my number one strategy for staying ahead and on top of course work without falling behind. By beginning my reading ahead of schedule,

I was often finished with a 10-week program within a period of 3 to 5 weeks. This left me with only copying and pasting my homework to the course room, uploading my assignments on the due dates, and responding to my peers in the course room. Sacrificing time upfront allotted me more time to do whatever I wanted. It also extended my breaks between courses.

2. Prepare a generic introduction. Throughout your program you will be asked in each course to write an introduction to submit within the course-room the first week of school. To cut down on the redundancy, I prepared a generic introduction about myself and the current course I was in. Then, semester after semester, I modified the section on what I am wanting to accomplish or learn from this course. It might not sound like a lot, but it saves valuable time, and this is what I want you to do—use your time wisely. A simple copy and paste are much better than re-inventing the wheel.

3. Bank your time. Most importantly, accept that you will have to sacrifice a couple of your weekends to complete multiple assignments during those days you set aside so that you can complete all your work ahead of time. This is a way to *bank* time—you work now to save time you may need in your future. Banking this time will be worth it because you will be prepared for the *what ifs* that are just going to happen in a busy adult's life. What if I get sick and cannot complete my work? News flash, it's already done! What happens if my child has a game? Guess what? You can participate because you worked ahead. What happens if I have a complex project to complete at work? No worries! This won't affect my progress in the course room. Why?

Because I prepared ahead of time. What happens if there is a family emergency? Still covered!

4. Don't let them tell you how to manage your time. You know better than they do how to best allocate your time. If your institution happens to be one that micro-manages the course room by locking you out of future course work, I recommend that you petition for them to unlock the classroom because you are supposed to complete assignments according to <u>your</u> schedule and not their ideal of controlling your work load. After all, there is no harm in working ahead of schedule; it will not harm anyone by doing so. At best, they should only ask that you delay loading your assignment until it is due, if you decide to move ahead of schedule.

As I suggested when you have your first interviews with prospective universities, I would ask this question prior to registering at a particular institution. If the university's policy is to withhold coursework by not allowing you to know what the assignments are and when they are due ahead of time, you should consider looking into another university's program that will honor their word to let you advance in a course according to your responsibilities and schedule. If you were attending a brick and mortar institution you would have free access to completing all assignments at your own pace; from the course syllabus you would know what the reading and writing assignments were; you could read and research ahead of schedule. Nothing would be withheld in a traditional classroom, so it should not be withheld online either.

STEP TWO

Strategies to Save Time

—————————— ୬౿౿ ——————————

Hopefully, you are beginning to see the benefits of my success with online learning just by getting tips from the introduction to the basic steps. I promise that as you navigate through the process, banking time will enrich your life. Following these strategies will save more than just your time because you can keep some form of consistency in your life. It is important to maintain a work/life balance with family, friends, and co-workers. We will discuss this further in detail later in the process when I share the importance of a solid support group

Now that you have reviewed your professor's expectations and the syllabus, you are ready to tackle the course-room workload. I know, this is where it gets real. It is also when you second-guess the best decision you have made so far because you revert to questioning if you can do it. I say, "YES you can!" and I will show you how. So far, you took a few minutes to handle the initial paperwork. Now the meat and potatoes begin. Proceed to your weekly course room work/assignments.

1. You should have a folder set up on your computer just for your course work. Begin by creating a folder in Word labeled with the course title, name, and date for the class you are currently enrolled. For example: Psych1600-Mental Health and Wellness-

4-7-2020. ***This step is critical:*** Why? Because you may want to revisit a prior topic in the future, and it makes it easy to retrieve later.

2. Now open a blank sheet in Word.

3. Log into your online course room.

4. Retrieve your syllabus

5. Go to Week One's homework.

6. Copy the title of Week One's course work on the blank page you opened in Word then paste.

7. Save the document by the corresponding course work's name. For example: U0a1-Why is Mental Health Important.

8. Go back to your course room online and copy Week One's work, then paste it into that same document. (NOT the assignment attached, steps will follow later).

9. You might have to clean up what you copied because of the format the school uses versus what is aligned with Word.

10. OK—stop right there. Let's get really picky now and then you won't have so many headaches later. This is a good time to pre-set your margins in Word. What font does your university require? Go to Home and click on Font. Most universities want you to choose Times New Roman, regular, 12. Before you say OK, remember to click on that "set as default" button.

Did you know that different universities require different margins on their assignments?

Yep. Some want assignments to be all 1" margins. Some want 1.5" margins. Some want 1" bottom margins and others want 1.2" bottom margins. Go ahead and find out now *and set your default margins*-NOW. When you go to Layout on your ribbon, click on your margins icon and choose custom margins. Set your top, bottom, left, and right margins. But the important step is at the bottom of that drop-down box—You want to click on the "set as default" button. This way, every time you open a new document, it's going to already have those margins that your university requires.

11. Now save it

12. Create a sub folder inside of the first folder you created above titled *"homework."* You will place this saved document inside of this sub folder labeled homework until you are ready to begin working on it.

13. You will follow these steps for all proceeding homework assignments.

14. Next, you are ready to create assignment sheets.

15. Open a blank sheet in Word.

16. Return to your online course room.

17. Copy and paste the title of Week One's assignment on the blank page you opened in Word. Keep in mind that you may not have an "assignment" for week one. However, this method will work for whichever week your assignments begin.

18. Save it. Example: *TLovejoy-Capers-U0a1-Finding Good Mental Health.*

19. You may also have to clean up what you copied because of the format the school uses versus what is aligned with your computer's default Word setting.

20. Now create a designated sub folder labeled *"Assignments"* inside of the file folder labeled Psych1600- Mental Health and Wellness--4-7-2020 from the previous page and place that saved assignment here.

21. You will save all scheduled assignments in the "Assignments" folder by continuing the preceding steps.

22. Whenever you are ready to begin working on homework/assignments, you will simply open up the named file and complete the week's work, copy, then paste or upload into your online course room when it is due.

23. **Important**- Do not forget to respond to your peers each week according to your syllabus. Not responding adversely affects your overall GPA due to the significant reduction in your grade for not complying. Learners have failed a course because of neglecting to respond to their peers according to the syllabus, although they may have past all coursework.

24. Inside the *homework/assignment* folders, make a new sub folder titled *"Turned In."*

25. As you complete your *homework/assignments* you will place them into the corresponding folders. These two folders will keep you on track by helping you to remember which assignments you submitted for the week and which one you still need to submit.

26. You will have all your folders and homework/assignments ready for the whole quarter!

27. Remember that generic introduction you wrote to use with each course? Go get it.

    a.   Create a new folder called *Introduction.*

    b.   Now copy and paste your generic introduction into the new folder labeled *"Introduction-4-7-2020."* You will now be able to modify this introduction for all upcoming courses. (this *introduction* folder will be a stand-alone file outside of the main folder so you can retrieve it for future courses).

Helpful Hints:

1. **Create a directory.** You can also create a Directory for each semester that catalogues exactly what can be found in each week's folder according to the topic and assignment that is due based on the title. A short sample is found in the Resources section of the handbook.

2. The directory can also aid in a quicker recovery should you need to review documents in your future work. Believe me, it can become overwhelming in a hurry when you know you may have already addressed a topic. Use what you've already written instead of re-inventing the wheel! However, you can do this only if you can immediately put your hands on it. Otherwise, you may have to re-visit the topic again. So, if you found a nugget of information such as a good reference you might want to use later, put that in the week's directory.

Notes

_____

_____

_____

_____

_____

_____

_____

_____

_____

_____

_____

_____

_____

_____

_____

_____

_____

_____

_____

_____

_____

_____

_____

_____

_____

_____

STEP THREE

Ancillary Tools

◦၄၄ၐ

1. Choose where you are going to work. I know this sounds rather simple, but you need a spot to write, read, and concentrate so that when you go there, your mind will say "Study." Walk around your house and find somewhere that has no real meaning to you, if possible. If you plan to work in a library or in an office building, go to the same spot every time. Humans are very territorial. Locations have meaning to us. You must choose a location that does not mean relax, eat, or sleep. Otherwise, you will find that your mind is otherwise occupied.

2. Multi-colored two pocket folders to store work.

3. A sharpie to label folders (example in resources section).

4. Select a safe storage place to house your folders because they will accumulate throughout the PhD program. One student I knew had a blank wall opposite her washer/dryer. She put up a long shelf with 2 brackets and a painted board. That became her personal desk. Even though it was in the laundry room, she had her back to the washer and dryer. That spot only meant "Concentrate" to her. Later she hung a wall file set above the desk. Another found a damaged door, cut it off and painted it, and

found two old 2-drawer file cabinets. The door and file cabinets became her desk. Yet another cleaned out a small closet, used 2 brackets and a wide board, and made a desk that could be closed off from prying little fingers.

5. **Important:** Your "Holy Grail" is the *Publication Manual of the American Psychological Association 7th Edition.* This book will be like carrying your Bible because it is your lifeline to developing and creating scholarly discussions and assignments using proper APA format. Always know where you keep this book.

A second important source for APA formatting is a book I used— *APA: The Easy Way! A Quick and Simplified Guide to the APA Writing Style* the 6th edition by Peggy M. Houghton, PhD and Timothy J. Houghton, PhD. However as of July 2020, this book has been updated for the 7th edition.

Helpful Hints:

1. Take the multi-colored folders and label them with your sharpie by the course you are taking. On the inside pockets label what you want to place in the left and right pockets.

Remember one side should house your weekly work and the other side should house your assignments.

2. Store them in your designated area within your home. It makes retrieval fast and easy. This is a great place to store your printed syllabus and the professor's contact information should you need to quickly access it.

3. *APA: The Easy Way!* is a great go-to when you find yourself having difficulty figuring out how to properly cite a reference. I found this handbook to be a life saver because it simplifies things in a more concise manner when I had questions by providing clear examples.

Notes

Notes

The Importance of a Solid Support Group

I will not lie or sugar coat the challenges that arise while taking a rigorous PhD program. It can become brutal. This is the reason why it is essential to align yourself with a solid support group. Your support group can consist of a multitude of individuals from family, friends, co-workers, or your peers.

However, you must understand that you will have to seek out like-minded people because most people cannot comprehend the gravity, the effort, or the grit needed for you to succeed in a PhD program. Many people will listen to you as you explain what you are involved in, but they usually are just being polite (as you will soon discover). You'll remember this fact when they abruptly change the subject of the conversation or when they do not engage in reciprocating the conversation.

While this might be okay in the beginning (because you may not notice their lack of interest or comprehension of the subject matter), you may soon begin to feel isolated. Another enlightening moment for you can happen when you find yourself re-assessing your immediate circle. Chances are, you may begin to realize that it is time to leave some people behind or temporarily avoid those people that you may have known for a lifetime.

This is because you are needing strength and support from those who have gone through what you are experiencing or are facing your same challenges. Your growth will become dependent upon individuals who are on the same level that you are, such as your peers. This is not saying that you think you are better than the people you leave behind. On the contrary, it merely signifies that your life is flourishing in a different direction. Because your experiences are so very different from the challenges you are facing, you may have outgrown these individuals and will need to choose to love them from a distance if they cannot offer you the support and solace you are needing during this very grueling experience.

Navigating a PhD program will test everything that you have. It is like being on a roller coaster at an amusement park that will not stop. There will be very low moments and high levels of frustration, followed by peak moments just like a roller coaster that reaches the top just before it falls over 60 miles per hour to the lowest peak. When these moments occur, you will need a lifeline, a person who can talk you off the edge and bring you back to reality so you can regain your sanity.

Yes, it is that severe and only the strong will survive. You will find yourself throwing a tantrum like a two-year-old as an adult because you have become so frustrated. The only remedy is to arm yourself with the proper tools and coping strategies to ease the stressors.

Just like many of my peers, I suffered through this embattled roller coaster. The one common factor that saved us was coming to terms that we had to take on a different perspective, one that allowed us to dampen our egos and to accept the reality that this was not about us but about the prescribed lessons we would learn once we freed our mines from *self*.

What is meant by *freed our mines from self*? It simply means that we had to come to terms that although we are students, this is not about us, but the lessons our professors are attempting to instill in us. Progressing through the earlier course work may not present as many challenges as those that present once you are in your dissertation courses.

At best, you may find that ineffective time management is a major problem, as it is with most online learners. I discovered after mentoring many of my peers that one common problem consistently arose, and it was time management along with the learner's desire to hurry through the coursework. As the trusted individual that they relied on for guidance, I found myself repeating the tips and tricks that I used to guide me through my advanced degreed programs with limited stressors. I did not say that I sailed through the programs with ease. I mentioned that I had limited stressors compared to surmountable experiences with frustrations.

This is the very reason why I decided to write this handbook. I felt that this advice can become a source of value for individuals who have a desire to acquire advancement in their profession without sacrificing their education. I feel it is important to share knowledge learned with others so they can accomplish their goals and dream. I want to help as many people as I can achieve their dreams so they, too, can feel that excitement and joy that I did when I first walked across the stage and received my master's degree and shortly after writing this handbook, my PhD.

I want others to feel that there is hope when they find themselves bumping into the walls and cannot see their way out of the darkness. I am here to tell you there **IS** hope and light at the end of the tunnel. The way to master good mental health is acquiring effective attack mechanisms.

When individuals modify their behavior, their realities can take on a new perspective. For instance, the use of positive psychology can be instrumental in whether a person succeeds or fails. Khan and Jahan (2012) discussed that positive psychology is the scientific study of virtue and strengths in humans. According to the researchers, positive psychology examines the development of a person to determine what areas of life are thriving and which areas need more attention to allow for improvement and achieve success. In her dissertation, I posited that positive psychology seeks to answer how people thrive and how the influences of positive emotions impact their well-being, behaviors, and performance. This method can also be applied to explain how positive psychology influences relationships, gratitude, and an individual's sense of self-actualization (Lovejoy-Capers, 2020).

Effective coping tools are essential to succeed and obtain desired goals. Whether you choose to rely on your faith, family, friends, co-workers, or peers the main point is that you need an outlet to alleviate your stressors. Kavar (2015) discovered in his study on spirituality and the meaning of self that intimate unique individual connectedness with spirituality provided meaning and a sense of purpose in life for people. Even if this means you have to take a break and hang out with your girls/boys, meditate, workout at the gym, shoot some hoops, or partake in a spa day, you must remember to partake in some activity that will create mental acuity.

Whatever the chosen method maybe, consistency is key. Do not wait until you are so frustrated that you feel like your head is going to explode before you carve out some me time. Delayed attention to the stressor will leave you with feelings of defeat and inadequacy. You wouldn't wait until 24 hours after you broke your leg to take a pain reliever, so please take care of yourself and take that time off before your body simply breaks down from stress and mental fatigue,

Unless you care for your mental health, you might retrieve so far into your head that often you can develop mental blocks that are hard to conquer. But learning how to overcome when things are not working in your favor, before they become overwhelming, is an effective coping strategy that you should hang on to. My recommendation is to develop these traits early to avoid falling victim to total mental and physical shut-down.

Helpful Hints:

1. It is okay to feel overwhelmed. It is not the feeling that will damage you, but the way you internalize the emotion. Just step away for a few hours, a day, a week (remember??? The reason for

mentioning a week is because you are supposed to be weeks ahead of the program by following my methods). I assure you when you return, you will feel refreshed. Not only will your cognitive acuity be crisper, you will begin to clearly see what is being asked of you and how to approach it from a different angle.

2. It is okay to ask for help. We may have a lot of experience and knowledge, but we do not know everything. You've never done this before! Asking for help is a sign of strength and moral character.

3. It is also okay to acknowledge feelings of frustration. Again, the recovery is what matters. When you acknowledge that you need to step back, you can begin that needed mental healing. The faster you recover, the quicker you can return to complete the work assigned.

4. It is okay to cry. Yes, I said, "Cry." But do not wallow in your situation. Acknowledge it, address it, clear your head, and move on. One thing that I did when I felt like I was becoming frustrated was, I sang and danced like nobody was watching. It freed my soul.

I smiled, laughed, and praised God for allowing me to embark on this wonderful journey even though I questioned why I was doing it.

Then, after my pity party, I snapped back to reality and hunkered down and began the process of focusing on the prize before me, earning my PhD. There were even times when I simply set the work aside and did not revisit it for a week. Guess what? I was fine and was still on track because I put the effort in early on to be ahead by preparing myself for the what ifs.

Notes

_____
_____
_____
_____
_____
_____
_____
_____
_____
_____
_____
_____
_____
_____
_____
_____
_____
_____
_____
_____
_____
_____
_____
_____
_____
_____
_____
_____
_____
_____
_____
_____
_____
_____

Preparing to Select Your Research Topic

─────────── ꙮ ───────────

The pitfalls that my peers and I discovered during this process were challenges with selecting the right research topic. Part of the reason for these difficulties was because we were all wide-eyed and green with the heroic fantasy of wanting to save the world. What we learned, some of us quicker than others, was that there was no need to make the experience of research complicated. When I say complicated, I mean one of the best means of conducting your dissertation research is to piggy-back on current studies that already exist. You have a ready-made reference list to begin your own research.

You might begin this process by reviewing recent dissertations that have been published on your general topic of interest to see what the findings and limitations were in the study and what their recommendations were for future research. If you have a professor who shares your topic of interest, go to ProQuest Dissertation and Theses and search for dissertations in which they were mentors or committee members. You search by their name, not by the title or the writer's name. This may give you some ideas on dissertations to read.

The beauty of taking this approach is that the literature is there, and you can review dissertations that align with your theory and develop the research further. I wish I had listened to my academic advisor who told me early on not to re-invent the wheel.

However, I was so turned around trying to navigate the process that my topic changed more than I can remember. I soon learned that this became a major problem when it came time to complete my comps. Because my research topic changed so much, I became confused and could not recite what my actual research question had become without saying, "Hold on," or I simply stumbled over what it was.

This was a problem that I did not foresee because when comps came, I had to prepare another literature review from scratch. The literature I had read no longer corresponded with the research question that had gradually evolved. I wanted to pull my hair out! I knew something was wrong, but I was so caught up in the process, I never stopped to address the differences in my research and my research question. Not addressing the issue increased my frustrations and confusion, which eventually slowed my progression to complete my chapters. Luckily, my mentor realized that I was not addressing the correct research question from our last encounter in one of my Tracks we shared. If it had not been for him, I probably would not have progressed in a timely fashion and achieved the milestones that I have today.

I am sharing my story here because it is important to understand that our passions can often become grand, thus placing increased stressors upon us. It is okay to be passionate about a topic, and realistically you must be because you will be eating, sleeping, and dreaming about your dissertation; but most importantly, you have to be practical. You must be practical about selecting a research topic that you can live with over the next few years, and you must be patient. You can start with a general idea, but it must become very narrow to be manageable.

Doctoral candidates tend to place unrealistic time limits on when they will finish their programs. What I discovered is that these time limits create an added sense of pressure that increases stress levels because you missed your self-imposed deadline. The program is already rigorous and comes with many complexities; the last thing you need is additional stress that can affect your mental acuity.

This is why I mentioned that you must have patience, the patience of Job. There will be times when you submit parts of your chapters, and you think it is some of your best work, but it is returned with many edits. Now your ego is bruised. What do you do?

I say this with love—get over yourself! Although you are the one who pursues the degree, it is all about what your mentor and committee members say is right. In the beginning you will fight and become adamant that you will take a stance. I promise this will only lead you down a path of misery. They are there to help you by pointing out any weak spots that will help your research be stronger. It isn't <u>you</u> they are criticizing; it's just a word choice, a phrase that needs some tweaking, or a statement that needs to be strengthened.

Taking the "I'm going to show you" type attitude will only prolong the inevitable. You will lose! As a mentor to other doctoral candidates, I have had to talk a few off the ledge. The best advice I can offer is to take some deep breaths, walk away from the material, relax, go get something to eat, then return, even if it is the next day, to revisit the feedback. Because nine times out of ten you allowed your ego to overtake a critical teaching opportunity that your mentor or committee member was attempting to impart.

Helpful Hints:

1. Remember it is not them against us. Your mentor and committee member really do have your best interest at heart even though they may not be nurturing. <u>They want you to be a success.</u> If you have peers who are ahead of you in the process, take some time to pick their brains. Oftentimes, I have found that colleagues who are further along in the program usually have useful information to assist you with avoiding other pitfalls that might populate during

your research topic selection. They remember their trials and hardships and will gladly come to your rescue.

2. Do not get wrapped up with setting unrealistic time limits for yourself because you will drive yourself crazy.

3. **Just Breathe!**

Inhale

Exhale

Inhale

Exhale

Relax

Relax

Relax

Notes

_____
_____
_____
_____
_____
_____
_____
_____
_____
_____
_____
_____
_____
_____
_____
_____
_____
_____
_____
_____
_____
_____
_____
_____
_____
_____
_____
_____
_____
_____
_____
_____

STEP SIX

The Research Topic

--- ༻༄༺ ---

A t Capella University, learners are provided with three tracks to assist with writing their Dissertation Research Plan (DRP). During the initial track, you toss around ideas for a research question based on the topic you were planning to investigate. Learners work closely with their professor off-site for three days to develop their research question. Once they tweak the research question, they begin working on the DRP.

Initially, in Track One the learner and mentor discuss the research topic, the significance of the study, the problem, background of the problem, explain the research question, define the terms used in the DRP, discuss the purpose of the study, the methodology, and the dissertation title. During Track Two, learners explain how their study can advance scientific knowledge and determine the theoretical and practical implications of the study. In Track Three learners describe their research design population sample, ethical considerations, data collection, data collection procedures, the guiding interview questions, data analysis, the role of the researcher, credibility, dependability, and transferability.

Sometimes learners must tweak their research question to suit the research study. They may begin their research and discover that they want to take another path on that subject. However, once they have crafted a strong question for their study, the next step is to determine which research methodology fits best, qualitative, or quantitative? The subject you have chosen to research will very often determine this for you.

When you have determined what your research question is and which methodology is best for your research study, it is time to conduct a literature review. This is the time to develop a thorough literature review because it will become part of your comprehensive exam. Keep in mind that each university has its own set of rules that pertain to the comprehensive exam that could be modified at any time.

Helpful Hints:

1. Make sure that you select a research topic that you are in love with, because you will have to live with the subject matter for years.

2. Prior to selecting your research topic, see what the literature says before confirming your selection.

3. Review published dissertation as well; this can also let you know how much literature is available for your specific topic. Remember, if there is very little research available, you may have difficulty with the topic.

4. When considering your topic, you could also review what is trending in the world, then explore the literature that aligns with that subject.

5. Remember that curricula change, and you must act accordingly.

Notes

_____
_____
_____
_____
_____
_____
_____
_____
_____
_____
_____
_____
_____
_____
_____
_____
_____
_____
_____
_____
_____
_____
_____
_____
_____
_____
_____
_____
_____
_____
_____
_____
_____

Notes

STEP SEVEN

Comps

〜〇〇〜

At this juncture you are about to embark on achieving another milestone in your academic career. Every university has its own version of what the comprehensive exams consist of. At Capella University, learners use the information from their Dissertation Research Plan (DRP), which is the focus of their research question for the dissertation. It is advantageous to thoroughly go through your DRP early on, if this is applicable, to make certain that your plan will align with how you are going to investigate the research question after you have passed the comp exam.

Helpful Hints:

1. Make certain that your literature review is solid; you should be aware of the appropriate theories and concepts that align with your research question.

2. A literature review is pages upon pages of past research that demonstrates your understanding of the topic, why it exists, and if there are gaps that can be filled by conducting your study.

3. Neglecting to prepare a strong literature review will lead to challenges with proving that there is a need for your study.

4. Essentially, you are writing an annotated bibliography on steroids.

5. Review proper APA format.

6. Make sure you have compiled a good working reference list.

There will be many edits to your DRP, so you want to create a folder titled DRP with the date you created it. As you make revisions, always label the new edit by name and date. You will build on your versions. You will NOT revert back to an older version when making new edits. When you get a copy back from a mentor, a committee member, or an editor, save that version with a new name. That will be the one you work from. This way, each version will contain every change from the previous one. However, if you have dated each revision, if you need to look back to a previous version for some reason, it will be easy to retrieve. Also, as the work increases, our minds tend to become forgetful, so keeping the versions in chronological order can be helpful.

Notes

_____
_____
_____
_____
_____
_____
_____
_____
_____
_____
_____
_____
_____
_____
_____
_____
_____
_____
_____
_____
_____
_____
_____
_____
_____
_____
_____
_____
_____
_____
_____
_____
_____
_____
_____
_____
_____

Notes

_____
_____
_____
_____
_____
_____
_____
_____
_____
_____
_____
_____
_____
_____
_____
_____
_____
_____
_____
_____
_____
_____
_____
_____
_____
_____
_____
_____
_____
_____

STEP EIGHT

IRB Approval

⸻ ꙅꙅꙅ ⸻

Acquiring Institutional Review Board (IRB) approval is dependent on the institution you are attending and its policies and procedures that must be followed. Basically, what you are seeking is the permission of the IRB board to move forward with your research study. At this stage, you want to review your IRB guidelines thoroughly. This way, when you begin your IRB application, you will be well versed in how to appropriately follow each step required of you.

This is also an appropriate time to determine how you plan to conduct your qualitative or quantitative research study. Regardless of whether you plan to employ face-to-face interviews, interviews by Skype, Zoom, or some other media outlet, survey, journal, or picture method, you must be prepared to explain all of the factors that will safely guard your participants during your data collection process. Each medium has its own set of rules that you must adhere to. Therefore, after you receive IRB approval to move forward with your study, be aware of these rules before you begin the interview process.

I will not go into this in-depth other than to remind you that you must address informed consent and the methodology you plan to use to obtain your data. You will also discuss how you ensure your participants' safety and privacy during your study. Also, as part of the IRB process, you will have to communicate how you plan to maintain the gathered data and keep it safe for the required period of time according to your IRB board.

Helpful Hints:

1. Your program should have all information you will need for the IRB process readily available in the resources section of the dissertation process.

2. In between your breaks from your general courses, take some time to review the information to become familiar.

3. If you are going to begin the process of reviewing upcoming work pertaining to your dissertation, please take a week for yourself to do something totally unrelated to your schoolwork. Then use the second week to review the upcoming quarter so that you can use the third week to regroup prior to the start of your next semester.

4. It is important for you to keep in mind that over time the university might modify the requirements based on new emerging information that will aid the learners to improve upon their skill set in the dissertation process.

Notes

_____
_____
_____
_____
_____
_____
_____
_____
_____
_____
_____
_____
_____
_____
_____
_____
_____
_____
_____
_____
_____
_____
_____
_____
_____
_____
_____
_____
_____
_____
_____
_____

Notes

STEP NINE

Dissertation Course Room

────────── ๖๏๖ ──────────

Congratulations! You have achieved a major milestone in your life so give yourself a great big hug and do a happy dance. No, really, dance like there is nobody watching. It is exhilarating!

Now is the time to put in some serious work, time, and effort. It is the beginning of a pivotal moment in your perspective career.

Helpful Hints:

1. Pace yourself. Think of this as a marathon. Don't rush but keep a steady pace instead.

2. Do not place unrealistic deadlines upon yourself, it will create unnecessary stress.

3. If you have prescribed limitations that support the need for special accommodations, make sure you are aware of your universities policy of how they will provide the proper assistance to help you succeed in your academic career.

4. Keep your mind focused on the topic! Quite often learners can get bogged down with a multitude of ideas that float around in their

minds and although it sounds good to them, it actually causes them to stray off topic, which creates confusion and equates to developing an unorganized chapter.

Some writers put a poster on the wall in front of their favorite writing place. The poster simply states the research question. That's all. It can keep you from going down a rabbit hole.

5. Find yourself a go-to person you can discuss ideas with or someone you feel comfortable with when you simply need to let go of your frustrations. The sooner you re-group and regain mental acuity, the sooner you will be on your way to develop a more concise and thorough dissertation chapter.

6. Schedule breaks. It is critical to take many breaks as you are developing your dissertation. Often times learners get wrapped up in the flow and do not want to stop writing. What should be done in this instance to pace yourself is this: Once you get to a place where you can complete a thought, this is an opportune time to take that break or else you will pay later when you try to return to that discussion.

7. Know that it is okay to take a day or two off to RELAX! You must take a holistic approach to taking care of yourself to maintain your overall psychological wellbeing.

    Schedule time to engage in activities with your family, friends, co-workers, and yourself.

    Binge watch your favorite television shows.

    Take long walks and become one with nature.

    Whatever relaxes you, just do it!

Notes

_____
_____
_____
_____
_____
_____
_____
_____
_____
_____
_____
_____
_____
_____
_____
_____
_____
_____
_____
_____
_____
_____
_____
_____
_____
_____
_____
_____
_____
_____
_____
_____
_____
_____
_____
_____

Notes

STEP TEN

Organizing Your Research Material

─────────⟲⟳─────────

Finally, it's time to actually begin to write. However, achieving success during this particular stage is dependent upon maintaining effective organizational tools. It is essential to create detailed labeled and dated folders because there will be a lot of back and forth. If this step is not completed, you will quickly become very confused about the placement of documents and material that you have collected over the years while you have been working on your dissertation.

These are the steps to follow in Word:

1. Begin by creating a main folder entitled

    Dissertation Folder

2. Inside your dissertation folder, you will set up folders for each chapter. Make a separate folder for each of the five chapters.

    Chapter One/Date, Chapter Two/Date, Chapter

Three/Date, etc.

3. Inside your chapter folder, you will have several sub-folders.

   Why multiple folders? The answer to this question is because there will be many edits to each chapter. In fact, there will be more edits than you can imagine. To maintain control of all of your edits in each chapter folder you will start out with Chapter1-version1 as your first edit. After this is submitted to your mentor and feedback is provided, you will label the return chapter, chapter1-version 2. You will continue this process from all submitted versions after you receive feedback from your mentor. But remember, when you get chapter1-version 2 back, work from that version. You never work on a previous version again.

   Chapter One Versions=

   Inside this chapter version folder, you will gradually accumulate the following documents:

   Chapter One Draft

   Chapter One Version 1

   Chapter One Version 2

   and so on....

4. You will also have folders for the following:

   References

a. Although there are many programs that will house your references, most of them have troublesome drawbacks. I found it quite helpful to create a document called References, along with the date that reference list was begun. This way if I forget to include an author or reference, I can easily copy and paste it in while I was working on my dissertation without having to pull up another program.

b. You will also create folders for Grammarly and the one you'll be most proud of, your final edited copy.

When you have completed Chapter One, make a copy of your list of references.

References (next chapter)

Place it in your new Chapter Two References Folder and give it the new date when you began adding new references to Chapter Two. This process will continue for remaining chapters.

Literature Articles for my Study

During classes, your professor may mention articles and books that might be helpful in your research. If so, record them in this folder so that when you begin to write your dissertation, you'll have more leads on research to review.

Final Edited Chapter One

This is where you place the final version that you submit in the assignment area for grading.

It is equally important to label this document as such: TLovejoyCapers-Dissertation Chapter One-4-7-2020. You will repeat this step for all remaining chapters.

Helpful Hints:

1. When creating your reference list divide it up into two different sections. The first section will include all of the references that you have used in your references. The second half should be labeled references I might use in another area.

2. It can be helpful to include the page where you inserted your in-text citation to make it easier to find on your list. Also, take time to bold words so they will stand out for easy retrieval (just remember to remove the bolding for your final copy.

Example:

> Pieterse, A. L., Carter, R. T., & Ray, K. V. (2013**). Racism-related stress, general** life stress, and psychological functioning among Black American women. *Journal of Multicultural Counseling & Development,* 41(1), 36-46. doi:10.1002/j.2161-1912.2013. 00025.x

OK—here's another timesaver that can keep you from tears later on. **Right now**, the very first time you list your reference, do it right!!! Don't leave anything out or you'll have to go back and dig it out later. **DO** include all the information. And that includes the volume, issue, and page numbers <u>and</u> the DOI or website address. Use the website address only as a last resort.

This is very important. Many students use their university's library when doing research. As a result, for example, a Capella student may copy this address for their article, because that's what's at the top of the article: https://doi:org.library.capella.edu/10.1093/jcr/ucx74

You cannot use that website address. Remember this or weep later. If your address has the name of your university in the website, that means **ONLY** faculty, staff, and students will be able to use the website. Anyone else will just get a message to log on with your university ID and other researchers don't have an ID from your university.

Instead, you will need to copy the name of the article, put it into a search engine, and look for the DOI or website address that is found by clicking on one of the sites that show that article. Usually there are several. The researchgate.net site is good because it clearly lists the title, date, volume, issue, page numbers and the DOI.

A hint—often the website does have that DOI buried in there—see the letters DOI? and the sequence beginning with the 10? The DOI is the following: doi:10.1093/jcr/ucx74

3. Grammarly is a great tool to help with editing outside of a professional editor. However, keep in mind that Grammarly and Spellcheck in Word often conflict on which way to correct certain grammatical errors. Be careful before you make the change by reading over it first to see if it makes sense. Grammarly has a bad habit of recommending a word that is too casual for use in a dissertation. It will also caution you about using passive voice, but there's nothing wrong with using passive voice if you use it sparingly to change up word patterns and make the sentences more interesting.

4. Recite Works (reciteworks.com) is an awesome tool to check and verify that you have included all of your in-text citations, and that they match the reference list created. You can use it after you've competed each chapter.

When you get into Reciteworks, you will upload your manuscript. You will then have a choice of viewing your in-text citations or your references. For a single chapter, all you are concerned with is your in-text citations.

Recite Works does have a few flaws that I have found. If your reference continues from one page to other page, Recite Works thinks it is another reference. Not only will it think it is two different references, it will also indicate that it is not found in your document. Never delete a reference until your manuscript is completely finished for the last time.

It won't know if you've misspelled a name, so if you have written Clark in your in-text citation but write Clarke in your references, it will tell you there is no reference.

It doesn't understand dates. Therefore, if you say that according to the census in 2018, . . . it begins looking for the author that goes with that date.

One really helpful thing it tells you is when you should be using et al. (in APA 7th edition, if you have 3 or more authors, you use et al. even with the very first citation).

Notes

Notes

STEP ELEVEN

The Interview Process

T he most important aspect of the interviewing process that is not often shared is how to capture in-depth information from your participants.

The first thing you will need to remember is to craft well thought-out questions so you can obtain quality data. Also, practice by performing mock interviews to become comfortable when performing your interviews with participants. It takes skill to listen, process what is being said, and then to turn that information into follow-up questions, while still being focused on what the participant is communicating.

Try to focus on key phrases to use during the interview process because you do not write down anything during the interviews, and this is a challenge. Guess what—this is only the beginning, because as you ask those follow-up questions, you may have even more questions to the original follow-up question, and you have not even asked all of the follow-up questions from the first question.

It really isn't about how many interview questions you have created for your list. The purpose of the guiding questions is for reliability in the data. You want every one of your participants to respond to the same basic set of questions. However, it is all about the follow-up questions that you must ask, based on what the interviewee is communicating to you. You can develop five great questions and from those you ask, you can acquire quality follow-up questions that assist with answering your research question. The key is learning how to pull this information from each participant.

For Example:

- **Participant:** When I was working in corporate America in the management field, it was really difficult being a woman.

- **Researcher:** I heard you mention that it is difficult being a woman in corporate America. Can you tell me more about the difficulty you are referring to and how these difficulties relate to your experiences?

- **Participant:** I can remember feeling really saddened by my experience.

- **Researcher:** You have expressed feelings of being sad...What were you thinking when these sad feeling emerged?

- **Participant:** When I received my master's degree, I felt really proud of myself.

- **Researcher:** You just described being proud of your accomplishments with receiving your master's degree. Can you share what moments made you feel the proudest?

- **Participant:** Growing up I had so many people around me that influenced me to thrive despite my upbringing.

- **Researcher:** I'm glad to hear that you had many people around who encouraged you to thrive. Can you tell me more about these people who encouraged you to thrive?

Notice how I repeated what the participant stated. This method allows the participant to hear what they have communicated and gives them a chance to consider their responses while the interviewer is retrieving in-depth, rich, thick information by using the follow-up questions effectively. It is essential to get quality information because this is how you will collect your data. This data will be the basis for your patterns and themes that are necessary to write the presentation of your data section.

Helpful Hints:

1. Make sure you purchase two quality audio recorders.

2. Double check that you have, in fact, pressed the record button on both recorders. (You can select record and wait until you see the meter begin before starting the interview process. This way you guarantee that you did not just waste 60 minutes and have missed out on quality information. You will begin by giving the date, location, and time and the pseudonym of the participant.

3. If you are transcribing the transcripts yourself, it is a good idea to download the recordings to your laptop. This is because most of the audio recorders you will find do not allow you to press rewind and forward.

   However, you have the capability to do this when you listen to the transcripts from your laptop. The other benefit of having the recordings on your laptop is that while you are playing the recording and you need to take a break, you can see exactly where you are stopping and then upon returning, you can pick right back up where you left off without skipping a beat.

4. Downloading your recordings to your laptop also allows you to label your recordings by Participate 1, 2, 3,..., along with the date and time if you so choose to.

5. It also allows you to organize all recordings and transfer them onto a flash drive for safe keeping and back up, which is required for ethical and safety reasons.

6. If you are not a transcriptionist, I recommend using any available free services offered online or hiring one. Transcribing the interview transcripts can become very overwhelming. It also

requires a skilled ear to maintain the accuracy of what was obtained during your interview process.

7. Once the audio tapes are transcribed you will have to maintain a dedicated place to store the transcribed data separately from your informed consent files to protect the identity of your participants. Follow whatever regulations you receive from your IRB.

8. Be prepared. Your mentor may require you to critique your interview transcripts. The reason for this is to assess how thorough you are being as you obtain quality, in-depth, thick, rich data. Your mentor will also let you know what areas you may need to improve upon.

Notes

Notes

STEP TWELVE

The Dissertation Presentation

⸙ᥫ᭡

D uring this process, learners feel heightened anxiety because they are not certain what to expect. Many learners, including me, fear that the pre-data collection call or presentation (depending on your institution) is a platform where the committee performs a battery of military-style questioning. Some learners are so fearful that they begin to experience headaches, unexplained sickness, their palms sweat, or they just are a bundle of nerves.

Let me place your mind at ease, because this is not the focus of the pre-data conference call or presentation. Remember you are the *expert* of your study. You know what you've read and what you've decided on for your research. You are simply going to share this with them. The only goal that your committee is seeking is to understand your knowledge regarding your selected research topic and how well you comprehend the research process and methodology.

Usually, this step begins with the preparation of a power-point presentation. Prior to the preparation of the power-point, your mentor will discuss the sections and topics they would like to see included in the presentation and will tell you the length of time you should spend on your presentation.

Example of a Pre-Data Conference

1. Title Page

2. Research Topic

3. Research Problem

4. Research Question

5. Methodology

6. Data Collection Plan

7. Sample Population

8. Data Analysis

9. Theories Supporting the Research

10. Questions? (You are asking your committee if they have questions regarding your presentation).

11. Thank you.

When presenting your final conference call/presentation there are some slight differences. However, you will be able to use some information from your pre-data conference call/presentation for your final conference. This will save you some time and worry about re-creating the wheel. This example illustrates the difference between the two conferences/presentations.

Example of Final Conference

1. Title Page

2. Introduction

3. Statement of the Problem

4. Purpose of the Study (briefly state this—I used one sentence)

5. Research Question

6. Methodology

7. Results

8. Significance of the Study

9. Implications

10. Recommendations

11. Questions? (Again, this is asked of your committee members).

12. Thank you.

Helpful Hints:

1. Prepare to discuss where and what you see yourself doing related to your study in your personal future. **For example:** What profession you will apply your study to? Will you write a book or research articles about the findings in your study?

2. How is your study significant and can be applied to the real world?

3. Discuss how you will seek to expand upon your study by conducting more research.

4. Part of preparing your presentation slides is to *remember* to keep it simple and brief. Many learners tend to forget that a power-point presentation is not meant to present paragraphs but bullet points. It is the presenter who is responsible for telling their target audience about their subject. Think of each slide as a poster with lots of white space. Don't just read the sentences on the slide.

5. Practice your presentation ahead of time with a friend as your audience. Time the actual presentation and think up some imagined questions you would answer. That way you won't be wondering if you're talking too long, but at the same time you also won't find yourself through with your presentation with remaining minutes left in the allotted time frame provided to present your defense.

6. Your committee members are not looking for fancy. A few pictures when appropriate are okay. When in doubt just leave them out!

7. Be consistent. Use the same size font on each slide. Don't use several different fonts, bolding (other than titles), or italics.

8. Have someone else read the power-point presentation and check for typos. It's very embarrassing to see a title like this one, with your committee looking on:

"Form Interview to Data Analysis"

Form and from are two very common missed edits.

9. "**I found it very helpful to prepare a script for me to follow instead of having to look at the slides. The script that I prepared in advance allowed me to explain my presentation in a conversational manner, and this helped me stay on topic. At the conclusion of each topic I also noted in bold red **"NEXT SLIDE PLEASE."**

10. On my scheduled day to present, I found a quiet location. I also set up my script by placing each page in order from one end of my bed and around the next side. The only thing I had to do was read as if I was speaking and when I finished one page instead of fumbling to turn pages, I simply walked in front of the next page that I was presenting and continued my presentation. You could do this around a large dinner table or along your kitchen counters if you can be totally alone in the house.

11. Preparing your script gives you a chance to expound on your reasons for selecting your methodology, how you conducted data collection, and why you selected your chosen population, etc.

12. Just in case something might go wrong, I printed out my entire presentation and I dog-eared the lower right corners of the pages in case I had to reference a particular area.

Notes

Notes

STEP THIRTEEN

Formatting In-Text Citations— A Quick Reference

———————— ∂૭∂૬ ————————

(APA 7ᵗʰ edition)

Narrative Citation	Parenthetical Citation
Author (Date) reported . . .	(Author, date)
Author 1 and Author 2 (Date) stated . . .	(Author 1 & Author 2, Date)
If you have 3 or more authors: Author 1 et al. (2018) opined, stated, reported . . .	(Author 1 et al., Date);
If you have more than 1 reference in a citation, remember to put the references in alphabetical order (not chronological order).	(Brown & Green, 2018; Cherry, Garcia, & Cream, 2019); Gallon & Pint, 2008).

Formatting the Reference Section

Caution: As this book was going to print, universities are having to shift from APA 6th edition to APA 7th edition. There are quite a few rules changes as far as references go. By all means, find out what your <u>college</u> wants to do. Even colleges within the same university are going under different editions. You do not want to have to re-do your whole reference section.

Let's face it. There are many ways to mess up a reference entry. Please make a sample page so that you can quickly look at your model as you write a reference. Note where there are NO capital letters (in a journal article name or in a book title after the first capitalized word, unless it is a proper noun). Note where there are NO italics (in a journal article name). There ARE italics for the name of the journal or the name of the book.

The many <u>incorrect</u> ways to reference a journal article:

Vela, J. C., Sparrow, G. S., Whittenberg, J. F., & Rodriguez, B. (2018). The Role of Character Strengths and Importance of Family in Self-Efficacy. *Journal of Employment Counseling,* 55(1),16–26. https://doi-org.library.capella.edu/10.1002/ joec.12070

The correct way to reference a journal article:

Vela, J. C., Sparrow, G. S., Whittenberg, J. F., & Rodriguez, B. (2018). The role of character strengths and importance of family in self-efficacy. *Journal of Employment Counseling, 55*(1), 16–26. doi:10.1002/joec.12070

Journal article name—only first word and proper nouns are capitalized

Journal name—capital letters on all words <u>of four letters or more</u> and italics.

Italics on journal number only. The order is *journal number* (issue number), XX-XX.

Note the DOI—it cannot include the name of a university if you got the website while on your university account. You'll have to look it up using a search engine.

Here are examples of three different types of acceptable addresses:

https://doi.org/10.1002/joec.12070

http://www.apa.org/ethics/code/index.aspx

> Retrieved July 12, 2019, from https://www.merriam-webster.com/dictionary/discrimination

The way to reference a book:

If there is no DOI:

> Hoare, C. (Ed.). *The Oxford handbook of reciprocal adult development and learning* (2nd ed.). Oxford University

If there is a DOI:

> Brown, L. S. (2018). *Feminist therapy* (2nd ed.). American Psychological Association. https://doi.org/10.1037/0000092-000

Helpful Hints:

1. No matter how famous a person is, you do not include the first name of the author when citing their work. "Percy (2015) related . . . ."

2. If you have two references with the last surname, you include the first author's first initial in the citation. J. Smith (2018) said . . . According to M. Smith (2002) . . .

3. Ampersand (&) is never used in running text citations, only in parenthetical citations.

4. Et al. is Latin for <u>and others</u>. The actual Latin is et alia. Et = and. There's no abbreviation, so there's no period. Alia = al. AHA! Alia is abbreviated. That's why you put a period after al.

5. If you have 2 references with the same <u>first</u> author in the same year, you have to add an alphabet letter with the date (in the order of the reference.

    Vela, J. C., Sparrow, G. S., Whittenberg, J. F., & Rodriguez, B. (2018a). The role of character strengths and importance of family in self-efficacy. *Journal of Employment Counseling, 55*(1), 16–26. doi:10.1002/joec.12070

    Vela, J. C., & Warren, J. (2018b). Character strengths family self-efficacy. *Journal of Employment Counseling, 56*(12), 12–14. doi:10.1342/joec.13070

6. Remember there is no citing secondary sources for a dissertation. For instance, if you read a work by Lovejoy-Capers (2020) in which Price (2002) was cited, and you were not able to cite the original work of Price because you were unable to read it, cite Price's work as the original, followed by Lovejoy-Capers (2020) as the secondary source. Only Lovejoy-Capers work would appear in the reference list. For example: (Price, 2002, as cited in Lovejoy-Capers, 2020)

7. Always check with your institution's guidelines to see how they would like you to address secondary sources because rules can be modified without notice and what is not allowed today can change.

Notes

Notes

_____
_____
_____
_____
_____
_____
_____
_____
_____
_____
_____
_____
_____
_____
_____
_____
_____
_____
_____
_____
_____
_____
_____
_____
_____
_____
_____
_____
_____
_____
_____

STEP FOURTEEN

Computer Tips and Tricks

---- ꜱꙮꜱ ----

I talked before about banking your time and knowing how your computer can help you will give you quite a bit of extra time to bank! It's all about knowing the little tricks that are there for you to use. Many of us learn these tricks from others since we never took computer classes. Everything is learned by word-of-mouth. So, you may already know many of these tricks, but I'm hoping you'll pick up some new tricks, too.

1. Your Ribbon:

| 🖫 ⤺ ⟳ 🗁 ⩥ | Document1 - Saved to this PC ▾ | 🔍 Search |

| File | Home | Insert | Design | Layout | References | Mailings | Review | View | Help |

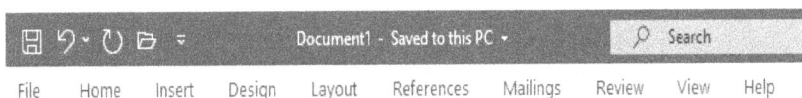

Your tool bar probably looks a lot like this, depending on what version of Word you are using. On a Mac, you should be able to find a similar set of formatting.

2. The "Home" Tab

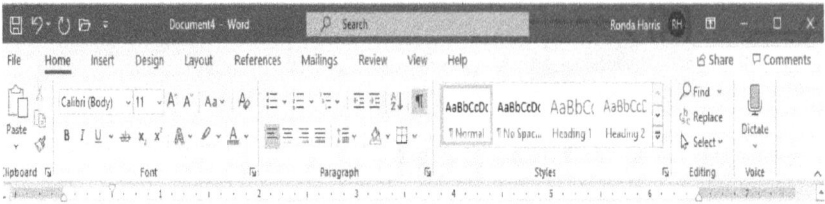

Your Home Tab probably looks a lot like this, depending on what version of Word you are using. On a Mac, you should be able to find a similar set of formatting.

a. **The font groups.** You're already familiar with the font group. Just make sure that you are choosing the font and size required by your college (remember that your college's rules may differ from that of another college, even within the same university). But do you ever use ?? The Aa is a time saver. In a reference, if you forgot and capitalized the words in a journal article, choose the whole article title, use the drop down to the right of Aa and click on lower case. All those capital letters will disappear. Yes, you'll need to put the first capital and those of proper nouns, but if you have a long title, it's great. Notice that you can also capitalize all or make all caps.

b. **The paragraph groups.** We use the paragraph group to choose a left-justified margin, but it's also handy to make quick lists and bullets. Don't do this manually when the computer does it for you!

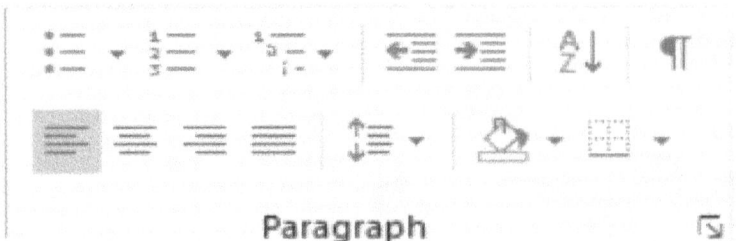

Paragraph

The first drop-down choice is for bullets, the second is for vertical lists, and the third is for outlines. A bulleted list is used if there is no hierarchy (there are no steps that are done in a certain order). However, if used often in a manuscript, they simply distract from the sentences that follow them. Type your first sentence. Then, click to the left of the first word, click on the bullet choice, and click on the symbol you choose. The bullet will appear, and you're now formatted for a bulleted list. Click on the end of the sentence, hit the enter key and you're set for the next item in the bulleted list. However, notice that the spacing and indentation is probably not correct. That will be addressed when we talk about your ruler and your paragraph choices.

The second drop down is for vertical lists. Please remember. A vertical list uses numerals. A horizontal list within a sentence is presented alphabetically. Therefore, you might choose from (a) a vertical list, (b) a horizontal list, or (c) well, that's it—I just wanted to make a horizontal list for you.

To make a vertical list, go to a new line on your page, below your last paragraph, type the first phrase, click just before the first word in the phrase, click on the numbering box, and click on your choice of numbering. In most formal writing, the standard is 1., 2., 3., like the following:

1. make a list,

2. check the indentation and spacing,

3. finish the list.

When you click on your numbering choice, it will pop up at the beginning of your phrase. Go to the last word in the phrase, click at the end of the word, hit the enter key, and you're ready for the next phrase with the number there for you. However, notice that like the bulleted list, the spacing and indentation is probably not correct. That will also be addressed when we talk about your ruler and your paragraph choices.

Another feature of the paragraph group controls the spacing of your lines. Some colleges and universities go strictly by APA rules—everything is double spaced. Others prefer single spacing for block quotes and single spacing for lists with 6 pt. between each part of the list. You may not have even noticed the little drop-down box in the lower right hand corner of the paragraph group. Inside the drop-down box you will find ways to set your spacing either before after a line, how to set tabs if you don't use a ruler. If you click on Line and Page Breaks rather than on Indents and Spacing in this Paragraph dialogue box, you'll find how to set the manuscript so that there are no widows or orphans. Widows and orphans are words or phrases at the beginning or end of a paragraph that are left dangling at the top or bottome of a page. You must have at least 2 lines of a paragraph at the top or bottom of a page. When you first begin typing a manuscript, if you'll click on Widow/Orphan control, you won't have to worry about that. <u>However</u>, always scan through your dissertation when it's complete, because every time you add or delete words, the position of the wording will change. The widow/orphan control takes care of sentences, but it does not take care of Level 1 and Level 2 headings. They can't be left dangling at the bottom of a page either, so you'll need to manually add spaces to push the heading to the next page.

When you use that drop-down arrow, you open up the formatting for all of your spacing.

For the body of your manuscript, your spacing should be 0 before and 0 after with <u>double</u> chosen for your line spacing. If you will set this when you first begin your manuscript, you'll be fine. You <u>do not</u> want extra space anywhere between paragraphs. If your college prefers you to use single spacing for a block quote, type in your quote, choose the quote and use your ruler so it will be block formatted. Go to the line spacing and choose 0 before and 12 after with single spacing. This will cause the quote to be all single spaced with extra space after the end of the quote.

For bulleted or numbered lists, do the same thing. This will keep your phrases single spaced, but there will be extra space between the phrases.

Another very helpful feature is the Show/Hide feature. Always have that turned on because it shows you every single key stroke including space bar hits, tabs, enter key strikes, etc.

c. **The editing groups.** The two choices I use here are the find feature and the select feature. You can also use Control-f and get the find feature. Either way, your navigation box will open.

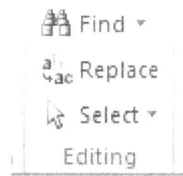

If you click on Find, you can choose from Headings, Pages, or Results. If you choose headings, all the headings in your manuscript are shown (if you are using the dissertation template. This is a time saver!) Need to go to your Chapter 1, Definition of Terms? Why scroll? Remember, you're trying to save time. Click on Definition of Terms in the headings list and you're there instantly. Compare your list to the template list.

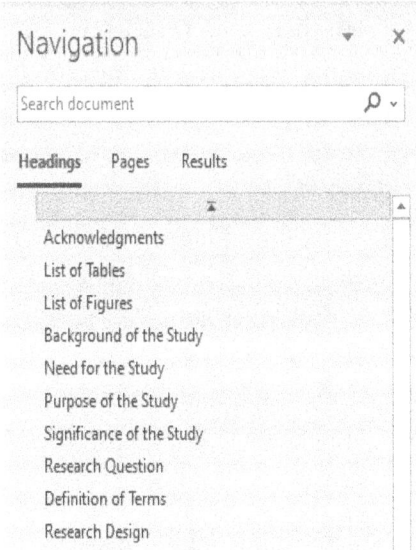

Your list of headings should match the list of headings in the template completely. Therefore, you can check this by comparing your manuscript navigation box and that of the template. Have you left out a section? Maybe it's there, but the section title just didn't get formatted correctly. When this happens, copy the title from the template and paste it over yours. Aha! The title will appear in your headings list.

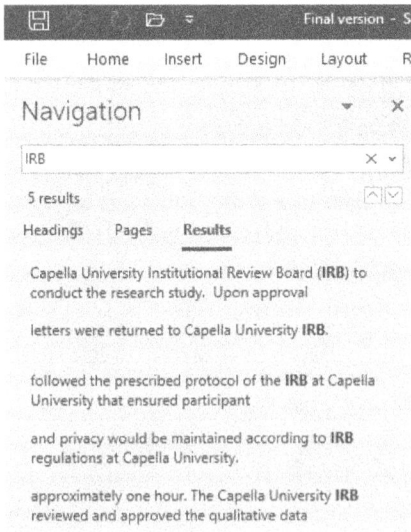

If you need to search for a word or a name, choose Results. Type in the word and every instance of its use will appear in the box. In this example I can tell that I used IRB 5 times in the dissertation, I showed the full name in the first instance, introduced the acronym, and then used the acronym alone in every other instance. If I clicked on that third listing, the computer would automatically send me to that page. No more scrolling page after page to search for something! It's also a quick way to search for an author.

One more part of the editing group I use is that last choice, <u>select</u>. If you choose select and the drop-down arrow, and choose select all, your entire manuscript will be selected. I use this if there are instances throughout the dissertation in which I previously highlighted my themes or patterns in different colors to check my organization and now I want to get rid of the highlighting quickly.

1. Select all (you'll see your pages turn grey),

2. Go to text highlight color,

3. Choose no color,

4. All the highlighting is now gone.

3. The "References" Tab

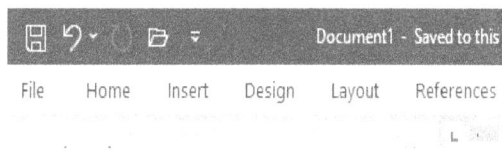

References. If you ever have a paper that requires footnotes or end notes, the Footnotes group is a dream.

The Table of Contents. The most useful part of the references tab is the Table of Contents group because this computer feature ties your manuscript to your template. If you use your template, your level 1 and level 2 headings are automatically tied to the ToC. That means you **do not** manually number your pages. Let the computer do it and change the numbers whenever you add or delete content in 4 easy steps.

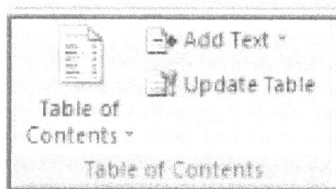

1. Click anywhere in the middle of the ToC. Your ToC will turn grey.

2. Click on References.

3. Look at the Table of Contents group and click on Update Table

4. If you have the choice of updating the whole table or just updating the page numbers, choose page numbers. Your page numbers are now updated!

4. The "Review" Tab

Within the review tab, you can look at a professor's comments. Notice that "next" choice. Don't waste time scrolling down page after page to look for comments.

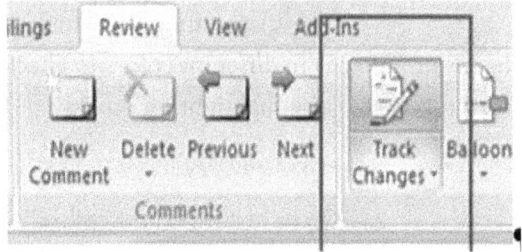

Simply hit the "next" icon and the computer will instantly show you the next comment that was made.

If track changes were used, you can switch from seeing all the edits to seeing a clean version with all edits hidden.

It·is·your·choice·to·see·this·versionone· (all markup)
It·is·your·choice·to·see·this·version.¶ (no markup)

5. Other Often Neglected but Very Important Tools

a. If your quotation is 40 words or more, you must use a block quote. But you certainly don't want to count 40 words. Do I count me as a word? It's so short. Well, your computer counts for you. Type in your entire quotation, whether it is a participant's comment or a quotation from a researcher, where it belongs in your paper. Highlight the passage. [I just did this beginning with If and ending in passage]. Now, look at the bottom left corner of your manuscript screen, waaaayyy at the bottom. Page 82 of 117   65 of 20285 words
I am on page 82 of 117 pages, and my quote is 65 words long. I'll have to use a block quote. This leads me to a statement I made about bullets and vertical list when I was discussing how to use your ruler.

You need to use your ruler. Many graduate students don't even know they have a ruler. It must be installed the first time you use it but should then pop up on your page automatically from that point on.

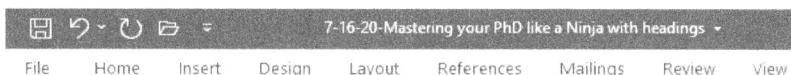

One of your options in the ribbon is View. Click on view and in the "show" group, click on ruler.

You can also add your ribbon by going to search, type in Show Ribbon, and your ribbon should appear under the ribbon.

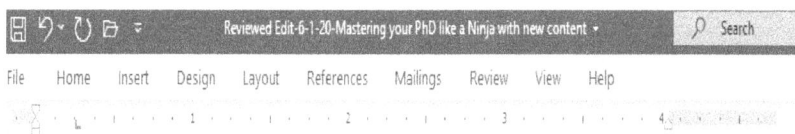

Viewing this ribbon, you can see my left margin set on 0, right margin on 4" and a tab for ¼". The arrows pointing at each other on the left margin are moveable. You slide them over to change your margins. For example, for a block quote your ruler would look like this:

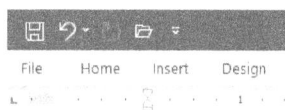

Don't worry if the arrows don't want to cooperate for you at first. You can drag the top one by itself, but when you drag the bottom one (the one that's like a roof-top) it pushes the top one along. Therefore, set the bottom one first and then the top one can be set where it needs to be.

Every paragraph must be indented, so by all means, when you begin your manuscript, set your tabs! You are NEVER supposed to manually space over to begin a paragraph. You must tab over. But when you set your tabs this way, you don't ever have to hit that tab key again. When you hit enter to go to the next paragraph, it will also tab over as it should Now there is a slight problem with this setting. EVERY level 1 heading will now be ½

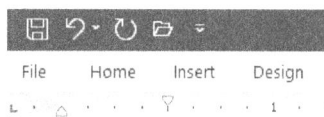

inch off. Click in the middle of the level 1 heading and move that top arrow back to 0. It won't affect anything else.

Bullets and vertical lists must begin a ½ inch from the left margin and the wording follows. For perfect lists, use that ruler! For some reason most computers automatically put bullets and numerals on the ¼ inch margin. Remember to always adjust bulleted or numerical lists so that the bullet or numeral begins on the ½ inch margin.

Your references must be formatted with hanging indents. You do not do this manually. Instead, you use your ruler. When you get to the end of the first line of the reference, it will automatically move you to the next line with the hanging indent. You learned earlier how to set your spacing. Depending on your college university, your reference list will be either double spaced or single spaced. If it is single spaced, choose single line spacing and 12 pt after. Your computer will automatically have each reference single spaced with a hanging indent.

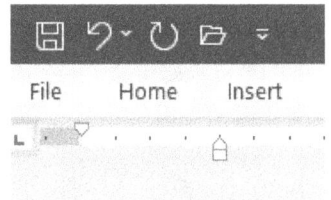

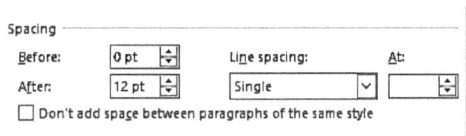

Tables and Figures

Tables and figures are very carefully scrutinized by your mentor, your committee, and the editors who have final approval of your dissertation. Please follow the basic rules of APA and you will have no problems.

a) In APA 7th, tables and figures are <u>left</u> justified. They <u>are not</u> centered on a page.

b) The title format is the same, whether it is a table or a figure (see the example on page 52).

c) There is no shading in a table. There is no color in a table. There are no italics in a table other than symbols used in statistics and in the name of the table. There is no bolding in a table, except for the table number.

d) Long tables may take up more than one page. In this case there is special formatting and rules that apply. Check your APA manual for examples.

e) Many colleges allow 10 pt font for tables. If so, be consistent and make sure that all tables in your manuscript are in 10 pt font. Only the Table number and Title are in 12 pt font.

f) Tables present information. They allow you to present much information in a very concise way. Therefore, you do not repeat everything in paragraph form that you present in the table. In the paragraph, you hit the high points.

g) There are **NO** vertical lines in a table. There are usually only 3 horizontal lines in a table. Here is an example of a table:

Table 1

Demographics of Participants

Participant	Age	Education
P1	55-59	High school
P2	50-54	Some college
P3	45-49	PhD
P4	55-59	BS
P5	35-39	BA
P6	35-39	BSN
P7	35-39	BA
P8	35-39	High school

h) There are 3 blank line spaces placed before and after a table or a figure to separate them more clearly from the paragraphs.

i) Don't forget that you must introduce your table or figure before you place it on the page. Table 1 includes the demographics of the participants. OR There were five themes and 12 patterns that were found in the data that were analyzed (Table 3).

j) There are times that a column in your header must have two sections. In this case, you will have an extra horizontal line. In Table 6, I have chosen to show gridlines in Layout. This is why you see the dotted vertical lines. It makes it easier to move the columns left or right if you need more space.

Table 6

Effectiveness of Professor Traits

Professor trait	End of semester		Start of semester		F ratio
	Typical	Effective	Typical	Effective	
Dedicated	4.706	4.789	4.154	5.000	19.26
Fair	4.000	4.263	3.731	4.667	575

The easiest way to create a table is to use Excel. Decide how many items will be in the header (in other words, figure out how many cells (the little boxes) you need across the table. For this table I needed 7 (there's a blank column between end of semester and start of semester). Then type in every part in a different cell by sliding the cell's right side over as needed.

Fill in all of your information, and copy the whole thing over into a **blank** document. That way you can play around with the columns. If you look at your ruler, you can see where each column begins and ends.

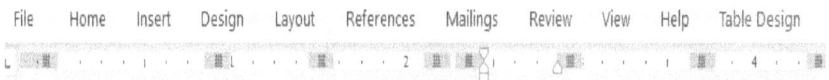

File   Home   Insert   Design   Layout   References   Mailings   Review   View   Help   Table Design

Highlight a column and slide the bar in your ruler, depending on whether you need the column to be wider or narrower.

While you are working inside a table, you'll see two new parts on your ribbon, Table Design and Layout. If you click on layout, you can choose View Gridlines and all the lines will show. This will help you because you can also hover over a grid line and a little marker will appear to show you that you can move that gridline up or down as needed. You'll need to practice this, quite honestly. That's why I recommend that you do this on a blank document. Remember that your table does not have to extend all the way across the page, it only has to be left-justified. But be careful, because it cannot go past the right margin.

Use your spacing from the Home/Paragraph group to make your lines of type closer together or farther apart.

When you have the table like you want it, copy it into your manuscript.

There are excellent examples of Tables and Figures in the APA manual.

Something else to remember is to keep a table or figure very simple and make sure that figure information is easily identified as far as years, weights, etc. Also, a table is a concise listing of your information. Therefore, you do NOT repeat all of that same information in the paragraph in which you discuss the table or figure.

You cannot copy a figure or table out of a book without getting copyright permission from the author.

Notes

_____
_____
_____
_____
_____
_____
_____
_____
_____
_____
_____
_____
_____
_____
_____
_____
_____
_____
_____
_____
_____
_____
_____
_____
_____
_____
_____
_____
_____
_____
_____
_____
_____
_____

STEP FIFTEEN

Things No One Else Tells You to Do

꒰ ଭ ꒱

1. Please, please read your college's publications that set out all the rules and formatting regulations you must follow. This includes the Doctoral Publications Guidebook and Doctoral Publications Formatting Guidelines. The Qualitative Dissertation Chapter Guide tells you what must be in every chapter. Therefore, there's no excuse for leaving something out. Also, pay attention to the template. It also tells you what must be in each chapter and <u>the order</u> in which you must present the sections and what the name of each section must be.

2. Read at least one other researcher's dissertation (depending on whether your dissertation is qualitative or quantitative). Ask your mentor or committee members if they have one to recommend to you as an example. And do not hesitate to read several if a particular section is giving you trouble (just read the section that's giving you fits!)

3. Check with your college on the use of first person. According to APA 7th edition, you **are** supposed to use first person when you are talking about your research. "I found that learners were very cautious when asked this question." However, the traditional view is that first person is not used in a dissertation (or only in the part of Chapter 4 when you are presenting your bona fides.) Therefore, you refer to yourself as "the researcher" or "this researcher" or find other ways to dodge the issue. Warning: Check with your college!!

4. If a paragraph or sentence feels strange to you somehow, read it aloud. Often you will hear where the trouble is.

5. I realize this is a tiny thing, but it's an issue that gets a negative comment from the Doctoral Publications Review. Pay attention to spacing. If you put one space between sentences, always put one space between sentences. If you put two spaces between sentences, always do so. It's your choice but be consistent. This is another reason to have your show/hide feature turned on. You can immediately see that you've put one space between some sentences and then put two spaces between others (or even two spaces between words). Yep, your manuscript is really going to get that much scrutiny.

6. Pay attention to the template. It will help keep you organized, because it has the different parts of the manuscript already set up for numbering, etc. Do not delete any section break from the template that you see. It's there to keep the numbering in the front section (Roman numerals) and the main part of the document (Arabic numerals) separate.

7. Use a page break (on the ribbon, go to Insert and choose page break at the end of each chapter. Do not use a section break because it can mess up your page numbering.

8. Because your template has your level 1 and level 2 headings tied to the Table of Contents, there is invisible formatting there that can give you all kinds of headaches if you aren't aware of it. When you begin typing inside your template, for example in Chapter 1,

Background of the Study, **do not put your cursor at the end of the word Study.** If you do, everything you type in that first paragraph will be formatted that same way as the level 1 heading and will appear in your Table of Contents. Look at your template. Begin typing where it shows [Paragraph text...].

For example, here are the first three lines of the template for Chapter 1:

CHAPTER 1. INTRODUCTION
Background of the Study

[Paragraph text is styled as Body Text......]

The template shows you **exactly** where to begin typing. The same thing applies for all other headings. Click below the level 1 or 2 headings right on the spot where you want the wording to begin.

Be aware that this applies to every chapter in your template. Avoid that invisible formatting or it will really mess up your Table of Contents.

9. Your Doctoral Publications Guidebook should be your student bible. It gives examples of tables and figures and covers every possible rule you can think of and lots you had no way of knowing existed . . . until you break them!

10. When paraphrasing, read the paragraph or sentences, look away, think about what you would say if a friend walked into the room and asked you what you just read. Then write that down. It will be much closer to your own words. You don't want to be bitten by the plagiarism monster.

11. Avoid anthropomorphism. Research can't see, data can't describe, and tables can't tell us anything. These objects have no eyes, no mouth, no brain. Talk about the researchers, the scholars. THEY did the research. The study didn't do it, the researchers did.

12. You'll also avoid a big no-no with the dissertation publication editors by avoiding passive voice. This also refers to a discussion of the researchers.

   Passive voice: The data were gathered and analyzed by the researcher when the interviews had been completed.

   Active voice: The researcher gathered and analyzed the data when the interviews were completed.

   In other words, put humans first. They did the work, so give them the credit. And vary your sentences by using "they," "he," or" she." Call them by last name or refer to them as the researchers or the scholars or the investigators.

13. While you are reading other dissertations or parts of dissertations, if you are writing a qualitative dissertation, pay attention to the verbs that are used. There's nothing duller than reading about every single participant who stated something, or every researcher found something. There are so many verbs to choose from— explain, suggest, share, said, stated, commented, argued, related, offered, considered, opined, confirmed, agreed, pointed out, noted.

14. Remember that you use past tense in nearly every instance. What the researchers wrote is over, in the past. What a participant said is over, in the past. The exceptions are when you are talking about statements that explain results such as "The emergence of social media platforms is a factor in relationship failure, according to a report by J. Brown (2016), and social media can be very addictive."

15. The following are just bits and pieces of trivia, but they are little things that can trip you up.

a) Don't use trademark or copyright symbols. If you refer to SurveyMonkey, you don't add a symbol for copyright or trademark.

b) There are no contractions used in formal writing (except when you are quoting participants verbatim).

c) There are words that you may find in the literature that you should avoid. Please don't talk about the <u>existing</u> literature. Think about it. Could you read it if it didn't exist?

d) Avoid the phrase "the <u>present</u> research" or "the current" research unless you have talked about the same kind of research 10 years ago and are making a point that you are comparing that research to the recent research.

e) The use of "present" and "current" is not used as a way to show that you are talking about your own research. Instead, use phrases such as this dissertation study, this dissertation project, in my study, etc.

f) And speaking of "recent," please don't refer to a study as recent or current when it's more than five years old.

g) Utilize is the darling word in many speeches and articles…but it's wrong. You use information, you employ tactics, you devise ways, etc. You use an umbrella to stay dry, but you utilize it to stab someone. Utilize means to use in a different or unusual way.

h) Don't confuse which and that. The use of which makes a noun very specific. The use of that is mainly just a connecting word. A quick trick: If removing the words with *that* would change the meaning of the sentence, you <u>do</u> want to use <u>that</u>. If you won't change the main meaning of the sentence, use which. Also notice that there is no comma to set off the phrase *that make lots of noise*. However, there ARE commas to set off the phrase *which are parked in front of the store*.

Examples:

Motorcycles that make lots of noise scare me.

The motorcycles, which are parked in front of the store, scare me.

i) To remember whether to use e.g. or i.e., just remember **e**xample—**e.g.** and that **is**—**i.e.**

j) The word "respectively" is used only when you have two subjects, and there are going to be two different objects in the sentences. The boys and girls wore blue shirts and red shirts, respectively. In other words, the boys had on blue and the girls had on red.

k) There is no, above, or below in a manuscript. You don't look above to see a table or a figure below. Above is the air, and below is the desk or someone's lap. Actually, it's because in professional writing, when a paper is published you never know where a table or figure will end up because it will be placed by a journal's editor. It could be on the next page. Just don't get in the habit of using the words.

l) You cannot begin a paragraph with a general statement such as "There are numerous articles available to researchers related to the interactions of perceived and experienced depression." This is an unsubstantiated claim. You can't prove that, just as you can't say anything that "everyone knows." This is serious research. You must cite who told you just about everything, especially dates and statistics.

m) You must avoid all language that is emotionally laden or that reflects your own opinion. Remember that you are the neutral observer. So, toss out words like surprising, believable, as you can see, interesting, it's clear, it's obvious, hard to believe, plain to see, evident, logical, there is no doubt, unfortunate, etc. You also do not refer to a researcher as famous, renowned, and other words of praise even if he is the number one in the world in that particular field.

n) Do not intermix the terms gender and sex. The difference between sex and gender is that sex is a biological concept based on biological characteristics, whereas gender deals with personal, societal, and cultural perceptions of sexuality. Your participants' sex will most likely be male or female. But when you think in terms of roles in society, you're referring to gender. Another way to check yourself is by seeing if the term is a noun or a pronoun. Male or female is used in this way:

The participants included 10 men and 12 women. (men and women are nouns.

There were 10 male participants and 12 female participants. (female and male are adjectives)

o) Don't know how to spell a word? Type it into a web browser as you think it's spelled…it'll come up correct!

p) Avoid mixing up **as** with **because, since,** and **for.** There is a difference in the use of **as** compared to **because, since, for,** etc. Because, since, for, and other words of this type indicate a linkage or causation—one occurs as a result of the other.

Here are examples:

I took an umbrella <u>because</u> the weatherman said it might rain.

<u>Since</u> I heard it might rain, I took my umbrella.

<u>As</u> denotes a specific event and there's a time element. I always think of the old rhyme "As I was going to St. Ives, I met a man with seven wives." You didn't meet the man from St. Ives <u>because</u> you were going there. You met him WHEN you were walking along that road.

Here are examples:

It began to rain <u>as</u> I was driving to work. Time is the key. It didn't begin to rain before or after, but during the time I was driving.

q) Your dissertation is going to be available to people all over the world to read. Your manuscript reflects who you are and is also a reflection of your university. This is why your mentor and your committee want you to do your very best.

Notes

WORDS OF
ENCOURAGEMENT

———— ༄ ༄ ༄ ————

D uring your dissertation process you might have to overcome some major roadblocks. Everyone will encounter their unique set of circumstances. Often, you may even have to compartmentalize them to meet deadlines. This can create a plethora of emotions and frustration that can lead to increased stressors.

In addition, you may also develop an inferiority complex, and you'll begin to doubt your ability to complete your program. These feelings usually emerge when you feel that you have had enough of the reiterative process of crafting a well-written dissertation. No matter when, where, or how these negative feelings reveal themselves, what matters is how you handle the situation. Thus, I have included some useful tools that I have used with my mentees to help them succeed in the dissertation portion of the doctoral program.

- Do not take anything personally.

- Feedback is NOT an attack on your intellect. It is simply a way to help you to enhance your work. I recommend that you make sure you are well nourished when reading feedback because most often learners miss out on the lessons being shared by implementing personal feelings into the equation, when this is not necessary.

- Walk away, then return to reading the feedback carefully, and you will see that what you originally read translates differently when you have cleared your mind. The attack that you thought was there has disappeared so that you can appreciate the critique.

- Remember why you decided to pursue your PhD, and keep your eyes on the prize

- It is critical to take some *me time*

- Don't succumb to imposter syndrome. Imposter syndrome is another strategic bondage method to keep you aligned with the beliefs that you do not deserve a prestigious accolade like getting your PhD. But you do, you will, and you DESERVE it!

- Believe in yourself. You are amazing and are built to endure, conquer, and succeed!

- Find a mentor in your program other than your university-assigned mentor.

- Create positive mantras to sustain confidence by repeating them to yourself in the mirror such as, "I got this, I can do this and I will, I am intelligent, capable, and I will defy the naysayers."

- Look at fear head on and know that fear is defeated when <u>you</u> get out of your own way.

- Even though you have yet not earned your PhD, declare it! For example, my friend and I addressed each other as Dr. and our names. It felt good to hear this when we spoke to each other. It sounds even better when it becomes a reality.

- Envision yourself walking across the stage and shaking the President of your university's hand.

- Meditate

- Pray

- Sing and Dance

- Remember the struggles that you endure today will create the memories you cherish tomorrow.

- Pace yourself by taking one bite at a time. When you attempt to do it all in one sitting you will find out that more mistakes are made that can only lead to more rewrites.

- When you feel that you are becoming overwhelmed, just walk away and come back to it. But always know that you can do this!

- It is completely okay to be selfish. This is your time, and you deserve to do something for yourself without feeling guilty.

- Sometimes you will not be able to prepare a home cooked meal, and this is okay as well.

- Sacrifice means unimportant things will be neglected. Oh well! There is always tomorrow.

- Ask for help from your significant other, your children, parents, and friends. Do what is necessary to maintain your focus to become successful.

- Roadblocks are just minor hurdles that make you jump higher to reach your goals.

- Most importantly, understand that there is light at the end of the tunnel, although darkness may cloud your path.

- Believe it, reach for it, achieve it!

  You can do this, you will do this, you will be successful with completing your doctoral program, and you will be called Doctor! Practice signing your name below. See how wonderful it looks.

Dr. _____

Sign Your Name Here

I know this to be true. During my 6 year and 9 months journey, I encountered unimaginable struggles that took me on an emotional roller coaster ride I was not prepared to deal with. During the beginning of my dissertation program, while attending my first track at Capella, my two brothers were in critical condition at the same time. My best friend's cousin passed away and shortly after that, one of my brothers died. Shortly after my brother's death, we discovered that my husband had a heart defect and had to have heart surgery. Following this, my father and mother-in-law were diagnosed with major health issues a week apart from each other.

My father recovered, but my mother-in-law died. I became a caregiver to him. About two years later, my father-in-law passed away, followed by my brother-n-law. On top of this, I became a support system for my only surviving brother who was battling major health issues. In addition, I became caregiver to a sister with a brain injury. Most recently, I had to endure the death of my only brother Dr. Johnny Lovejoy who had succumbed to his illnesses.

At the time that I was writing this handbook, I felt like I was still on this roller coaster that seemed like it would never stop. I had to deal with the reality that my role model, Dr. Johnny Lovejoy, had died during what is supposed to be the happiest time of my life. I forgot to mention that we are in the middle of a deadly pandemic with Covid-19 as I write this book to help you with your dissertation, and I will not get the opportunity to participate in my graduation, which I waited almost 7 years to do. I have solace in knowing that when I can walk across the stage to receive my degree that I will be doing it in his honor. I had to go through all these stressors while navigating my community advocacy, being a mentor to some of my colleagues at work, all while being a wife and mother of three. Having the responsibilities of managing a home and work is not easy. Although my children are adults, I am still a mother who understands that your job as *mom* does not end when your children become of legal age.

I'm sharing this story because I really want you to understand that there is no obstacle or circumstance that can deter you from accomplishing your dream of becoming a doctor. I'm sharing my story to show you that despite my personal challenges, I was still able to mentor several doctoral candidates and receive my PhD. It was not an easy path for me and at times I questioned why I was putting myself through this, especially in my 50s. However, I was determined to finish what I started because I believed in me. Even when I felt like I was on an island by myself, I relied on my faith and my motivation to keep me going on my path to getting my doctorate.

Although I had not signed up for the emotional roller coaster ride that I had to endure, I survived! I cannot say it enough that you, too, will meet your goal of becoming a doctor if you continue to believe in you. Hold steadfast to your dreams; this dream begins when you claim that you <u>will</u> become a doctor. I provided you a head start by having you sign the previous page. Look at it often to remind yourself why you embarked on this journey. Then, when your doctoral journey is at its end, why not sign your name one more time? It was so nice to see your official title-to-be the first time around, do it again when it's official!

This is your new reality! Own it!

I **AM NOW** Dr. _____

Sign Your Name Here

I am proud of your accomplishments. You have remained steadfast and took a gamble on you and guess what you won!!!!

Congratulations Dr.

You Did It!

Notes

WHAT OTHERS HAVE DONE TO REMAIN POSITIVE

---∂ᴒᴒᴄ---

I used meditation and long walks around the lake at my local park to regroup and to stay focused. I also have a glass of my favorite wine to relax. But what helps me to keep motivated the most is reading positive books like *Don't Sweat The Small Stuff...and It's All Small Stuff* by Richard Carlson, PhD., and being around my family and friends that support me. I want to say thank you as well for your support through this also!!!!

Dr. Linda Barbee

I engaged with fellow learners in the same process to vent and gain perspective. I worked in manageable daily or weekly increments to avoid burnout while still being progressive.

Dr. Angela Sartain

I just keep my eye on the prize and remember why I started this mission. I also look back at the hurdles I have scaled and the things that tried to beat me down and could not...that's when I smile and acknowledge I'm just an academic badass!

Greg Zar

My beliefs have carried me and continue to while going through this process. It's knowing I can prosper if I stay focused.

Rodrick Hollis

Notes

_____
_____
_____
_____
_____
_____
_____
_____
_____
_____
_____
_____
_____
_____
_____
_____
_____
_____
_____
_____
_____
_____
_____
_____
_____
_____
_____
_____
_____
_____
_____
_____
_____
_____

How to Resolve Conflict

-------⤳ ෙ ෙ ⤵-------

As individuals, we all have developed certain ideologies that may not conform to others. However, you must be willing to step out of your own way by checking your ego. Participating in a doctoral program is understanding that it is an ego-free zone. When you understand this as a learner, you will begin to alleviate a huge amount of stress from your life while undertaking a process that is already abundantly stressful.

Should you find yourself in dispute with a committee member, there are some things you must do to try to resolve the conflict:

1. Instead of going back and forth through emails, I suggest that instead, you should set up a phone conference. As you know, emails can further complicate a situation if a reader misconstrues the message that either party is attempting to communicate.

2. Talk out your concern with someone who you know will provide their honest opinion by remaining neutral and who will not take sides with either you or your committee member. Rather, this person should be one who can provide clarity and recommend whether to pursue further action or leave it alone and move forward. Remember that we can become so wrapped up in what we want to do that what is constructive feedback that could help you instead negatively impacts your judgment because you feel attacked.

3. Walk away from the situation and clear your head before you determine that there is conflict.

4. Should you encounter grave conflict that will hinder your progression through the dissertation portion of your doctoral program, you should have the right to replace a committee member. This includes your mentor as well. When you first talk with an academic advisor about attending a certain university, I recommend establishing how your university handles such conflicts prior to enrolling in a PhD program, because universities may operate under different rules regarding resolution of student/professor conflict. Ask where you can find this information in writing, locate that information, and file it away. Hopefully you will never need to use that information, but you must have that right to protect yourself if there are definite conflicts between you and a mentor or committee member. Otherwise you will be forced to work with that individual despite the conflict.

5. When students have their initial conference with Academic Advising at Capella, it is communicated that should the student have a major conflict with any of the committee members that cannot be resolved, the student does have the right to have them replaced. I would require your academic advisor to send you something in writing regarding your right to change a committee member because a few learners have been declined this right when they could not resolve a hostile situation. This way you are prepared to take further action that will result in protection of your best interests.

6. You'll find that everyone with a doctorate has their war stories— remember that your professors are human, too. They develop chronic illnesses, they pass away, they disappear for months at a time in Europe (yep, it happened). It may be that they will even give you the wrong information if they are not aware of grammar rule changes or changes in university rules. They may be under

pressure from their college to take on too many responsibilities (your dissertation is probably one of several they are assigned to at the same time they're working with you). Consider what is going on with them, too, as working individuals, but remember that you must be there for YOU. You must stand up for what is best for your successful graduation.

RESOURCES
Sample of a Directory

ꙮ

Week One: Psych1600-Why is Mental Health Important4-7-2020
Contains:
    1. A discussion on
    2. Citations from:
    3. I found a great article on (insert the topic) that I might be able to use in the research

Week Two: Psych1600-Implications of Negative Coping-4-7-2020
Contains:
    1. A discussion on
    2. Citations from:
    3. Contains assignment on *mental health*
       Example: I might be able to use the first two paragraphs in my literature review

Week Four: Psych1600-Methods to Selecting a Sample Population-4-7-2020
Contains:
    1. A discussion on:
    2. Citations from:
    3. Tips that one of my peers shared to help with looking up lit articles

Week Five: Psych1600-Methods to Selecting a Sample Population-4-7-2020
Contains:
    1. A discussion on
    2. Citations from:
    3. Helpful insight provided by my Mentor.
    4. Tips and tricks from the Librarian.
 	
You will continue this procedure for the remaining weeks in the semester and throughout the entire program.

** Note: The topics and dates in this chart are examples provided as samples. However, you will design the charts for your specific program.

Helpful Hints:

1. Include anything in this directory that will help you to effortlessly access information quickly.

2. Sometimes your professor may offer an article or two that they have come across which you might use in your study. It is a good idea to keep track of this information as well. Also, tuck away any interesting sounding article in your chapter sub-folder titled *Literature Articles for my Study.*

Example of How to Organize the Folders

Use multi-colored folders to organize your chapters

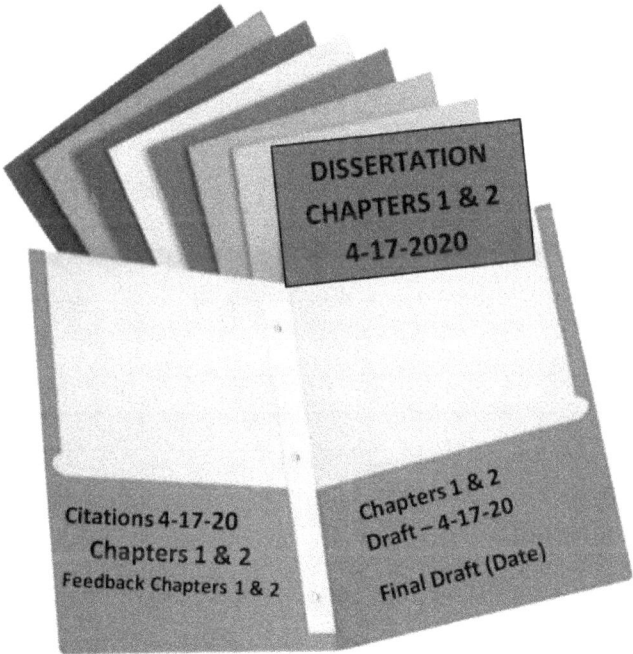

DISSERTATION
CHAPTERS 1 & 2
4-17-2020

Citations 4-17-20
Chapters 1 & 2
Feedback Chapters 1 & 2

Chapters 1 & 2
Draft – 4-17-20

Final Draft (Date)

Notes

Tools

───────────── ಶ ೧ ೧ ─────────────

1. **My Mentor**—My mentor provided me with a wealth of knowledge that helped me to successfully complete my dissertation. Often, my mentor shared a different perspective on certain challenges that I had to overcome while preparing my study. For instance, he talked with me about the different methodologies that I could choose from and why one was more effective for my study than the others. If I did not rely on his expertise, it would have taken me much longer to complete my research study.

2. **Librarian**—Your librarian can play a critical role in your success as you search for research material. In fact, they are the best resource when it pertains to navigating your university's catalog of literature articles. Librarians can assist with helping you format the key words to use to quickly retrieve the literature articles, which could save you time. When in doubt, reach out to your librarian who can also provide journals, articles, and books that are not readily available to you online.

3. **Recite Works**—Recite Works is an excellent tool to use to check to make sure that you have included all of your citations in the body of your manuscript that are also included in your reference list. Recite Works also allows you to receive a report that checks APA format of the sources included in your reference list.

4. **Grammarly**—Grammarly is useful to help check that you are grammatically formulating your sentences correctly. Although Grammarly is a wonderful tool but you must be cautious because I have found that its suggestions conflict with the spell/grammar check in Word. What I mean is that Word will correct certain words such as *was* or *were* but then Grammarly will turn around and suggest another way. This is because it's not human! It only "looks" at the words just before the verb. If the word ends in an "s" the program "thinks" the noun is plural even if it isn't. You can't beat human beings!! (Check to see if your university offer learner subscriptions for free prior to enrolling.)

5. **My Editor**—Ronda Harris was my editor, and she was amazing. What I really loved is that Ronda took the time to not only correct my grammatical errors, she explained why it was not formatted correctly by teaching me by providing an example. For instance, I thought I was being clever per Grammarly's directions by replacing the word *use* with *utilize*. But Ronda explained you use a bat to play baseball, but you might utilize a bat to ward off an attacker. Ronda was great at providing examples that were tangible to help me understand where I had made my mistake. Ronda is very nurturing, sweet, and fair. I highly recommend her for all your editing purposes. [And my editor added the following—her email address is rrh008@shsu.edu]

6. **My Peers**—My peers were an excellent source of information when I did not have a clear direction on how to accomplish a task within my program. Those peers who had acquired their PhD already were especially helpful because they had already fought the good fight and won. They became my source of inspiration when I felt that the darkness was too heavy to bare. So, make sure you form a circle of reliable peers who will keep you motivated and who will help you focus on your end goals.

7. **A Calendar**—A calendar is essential because they sync across mobile devices. They are useful to assist with keeping you up to

date on course work and assignment due dates. Of course, it can help with events outside of school as well.

8. **A Timer**—A timer is a great tool to remind you to take breaks to avoid burnout. You can actually use the timer on your mobile device since it is always at arm's reach.

Dissertation Consultations Available

Dr. Lovejoy-Capers is available to discuss the dissertation process for a nominal fee.

Contact information to request an appointment:

Email: tlovejoycapers@gmail.com

Please place in the subject line: *Dissertation Consult*

Ronda Harris is available to assist with editing your dissertation and to help with computer skills for individuals who need these services and charges a nominal fee.

Contact information to request an appointment:

Email: : rrh008@shsu.edu

Please place in the subject line: Edit Dissertation or Computer Skills Assistance

References

American Psychological Association. (2020). *Publication manual of the American psychological association* (7th ed.). https://doi.10.1037/ 0000165-00

Houghton, P., & Houghton, T. (2009). *APA: The easy way!* Author.

Kavar, L. F. (2015). Spirituality and the sense of self: An inductive analysis. *The Qualitative Report, 20*(5), 697-711. Retrieved from https://nsuworks.nova.edu/tqr/vol20/iss5/11

Khan, S., & Jahan, M. (2012). Humanistic psychology a rise for positive psychology. *Indian Journal of Positive Psychology, 3*(2), 207-211. Retrieved from https://www. questia.com/library/journal/-1P33561131091/ humanistic-psychology-a-rise-for positive-psychology

Lovejoy-Capers, T. (2020). *The experience of thriving among Black women following oppression* (Publication No. 27958969). [Doctoral dissertation, Capella University]. Available from ProQuest Dissertations & Theses Global.

About the Author

Tanya Lovejoy-Capers (a.k.a. TLC) is a native New Yorker, born in Brooklyn and raised in Manhattan. She now resides in Charlotte North Carolina, with her family. As a child, she knew that she was different. What she did not know was that it was because she had a passion for people. Tanya understands that everyone should be treated with dignity and respect no matter who they are, especially our elders. She loves listening to stories and learning from her elders. She feels that everyone should help others by sharing their knowledge.

Her belief is that we all have a moral obligation to reach one another to teach one another. This is the reason why she decided to write this handbook as a first-time author. Writing a book was not in her plan, but after mentoring several PhD candidates she discovered a common challenging recurring factor she found it necessary to address. Learners were overwhelmed with time management, organization, and self-care tools.

As an advocate, Tanya strongly believes that we all have a responsibility to share our knowledge to assist others to thrive. As a result, she decided to help PhD learners as much as she could by using her experience with her doctoral program by sharing her tips and tricks to achieve academic success. Tanya chooses to communicate through open and honest dialogue to demonstrate that through adversity learners can successfully prevail in their PhD program, as she has done.